Crash Start

Crash Start

The life and legacy of
Lieutenant
Richard Guy Ormonde Hudson DSC
Royal Naval Volunteer Reserve

by
CAPTAIN CHRIS O'FLAHERTY
Royal Navy

CP
THE CHOIR PRESS

First published in the United Kingdom in 2019 by
The Choir Press

ISBN 978–1–78963–062–6

CONTENTS

PREFACE

—◦⊙⊙⊙◦—

In April 2017 I was elected as the Royal Navy's Hudson Fellow at St Antony's College, University of Oxford. Having joined the Royal Navy straight from school, aged 18, and never studied at university, this was an immense privilege for a naval officer of 30 years' predominantly seagoing service.

My fellowship was financed by the Guy Hudson Memorial Trust. I knew nothing about this organisation beyond the academic fact that the trustees had considered (and accepted) my application, and that the trust would be paying my academic fees for the next year. So I started to dig a little in order to understand more about the origins of their generosity.

Having learnt that the Guy Hudson Memorial Trust was established in 1997 following a very generous bequest from the late Lieutenant Richard Guy Ormonde Hudson DSC Royal Naval Volunteer Reserve, I was disappointed to find that the only published summary of my benefactor's life was hosted on an obscure page of the Royal Navy's website and barely covered a single side of A4. I was conscious that he had bequeathed half-a-million pounds to establish the trust from which I was now benefiting, and thus I felt an obligation to repay his posthumous generosity by learning more about him.

After asking a few questions of the trustees, I broadened my enquiries by chatting with some of the regular attendees at the annual trust dinner. A longstanding professional colleague, the Honourable Michael Cochrane, then told me a few of the stories he had learnt about Guy Hudson, and my interest was piqued – Hudson was a brave man with a fascinating history. With the help of the superb library staff at the Royal Navy's Naval Historical Branch, I then discovered a few errors in his online profile (not least the date of his death!), and my determination to learn more about Hudson became a mission to research and script his biography.

Such was the genesis of this book. A man whom I have never met, and with whom I would never have become acquainted had I not been elected to the fellowship that bears his name, became the subject of my research and literary attention.

The volume that follows is the result of many intriguing hours of reading about aspects of naval warfare, legal practice and genealogy that I would probably never otherwise have investigated. It summarises the quiet life of a placid Oxford student who was thrust, fuelled by a patriotic desire to do his best for his country, into the front line of a vicious war. He became involved in multiple actions against the enemy, seeing things that cannot be unseen, and experiencing things that tattoo indelible memories on one's soul. Throughout the war he made many close friends, with bonds forged both at sea and in the wardroom bar. He conducted himself in combat with incredible zeal, initiative and bravery, earning the Distinguished Service Cross for his role in defending the eastern flank of the D-Day landings. In 1946 he was then tossed back into civilian life, away from the black humour and social camaraderie of the officers' mess.

Hudson qualified as a solicitor and started to earn a good salary, affording him and his new wife a comfortable life near London. But this material wealth could not ease the ingrained memories of war. He turned to alcohol for escape, often interspersing his day with a bespoke gin and tonic mix he nicknamed the 'Hudson Heart-Starter'. He was almost certainly suffering from what we would now call Post-Traumatic Stress Disorder. With his condition undiagnosed, his marriage collapsed, his legal practice was dissolved and his professional qualification was revoked.

Tales of sailors and women echo through history, and Hudson's biography is no different. Through his second wife he found salvation from his spiralling alcoholism; under her inspiration he quit drinking, re-qualified as a solicitor and made a significant fortune. Sadly, she pre-deceased him, and, after turning back to alcohol, Hudson died just seven months later.

The legacy of this patriotic, brave sailor now lives on through the Hudson Fellowship, which sees the annual assignment of a Royal Navy or Royal Marines officer to the University of Oxford, where they research and publish on topics of national maritime and strategic interest.

I hope that the life story I tell in this book does justice to Hudson's memory and gives inspiration to others to overcome their demons. And, as a fellow sailor, it is my thank-you for the opportunity he gave me to study at his former university.

Acknowledgements

———⊶⊙⊙⊶———

In writing this script I have been supported by many friends, colleagues, academics and also the committee of the Guy Hudson Memorial Trust, led by Professor Christopher Davies. Those who have taken time to aid my research are listed in the notes on my sources at the back of this volume; I owe them all a huge debt of thanks for their guidance, support and many snippets of information as I navigated the world of biographical discovery.

Inspiration for uncovering Hudson's family genealogy came from my mother, Elaine, who showed me how to explore the fascinating archives of various family history websites and records. I am also very grateful to the archivists and enquiry teams of Rugby School, St John's College (University of Oxford), St Antony's College (University of Oxford) and the Solicitors Regulation Authority.

Particular thanks goes to the three executors of Hudson's will, Mrs Sally Barbier, Mr Christopher Corfield and Mr Jeremy Lee, for taking consider-able time to share with me their memories of my benefactor. I must also thank Mrs Veryan Green, Guy Hudson's niece, for her time in recounting her memories to me, and for corralling her extended family into taking part in my research. As I investigated the naval aspects of his life I was assisted hugely by Ms Jenny Wraight and Mrs Kate Brett of the Naval Historical Branch, whose persistence in trawling on my behalf through volumes of records, to find the evidence of Hudson's bravery, allowed me to script with accuracy the more dramatic sections of this work.

As the script has matured, the graciously offered guidance of Kyla Manenti, Jenny Wraight and Harriet Evans has greatly aided the flow of my writing and has saved me from a number of errors of fact, grammar and spelling. However, any flaws or *faux pas* that remain are entirely my responsibility.

By way of contribution to the longevity of the Guy Hudson Memorial Trust, all rights and proceeds accruing from this book have been assigned to the sole benefit of the trust.

Chris O'Flaherty

Portsmouth, UK

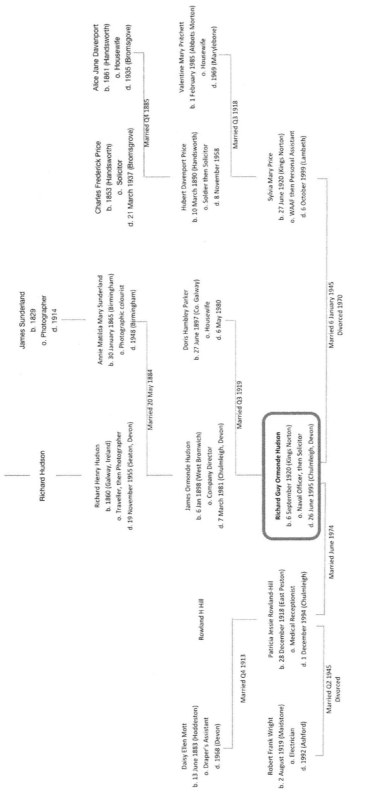

Richard Hudson
o. Lieutenant, 40th Regiment (2nd Somersets)

Richard Hudson

James Sunderland
b. 1829
o. Photographer
d. 1914

Charles Frederick Price
b. 1853 (Handsworth)
o. Solicitor
d. 21 March 1937 (Bromsgrove)

Alice Jane Davenport
b. 1861 (Handsworth)
o. Housewife
d. 1935 (Bromsgrove)

Married Q4 1885

Richard Henry Hudson
b. 1860 (Galway, Ireland)
o. Traveller, then Photographer
d. 19 November 1955 (Seaton, Devon)

Annie Matilda Mary Sunderland
b. 30 January 1865 (Birmingham)
o. Photographic colourist
d. 1948 (Birmingham)

Married 20 May 1884

Hubert Davenport Price
b. 10 March 1890 (Handsworth)
o. Soldier then Solicitor
d. 8 November 1958

Valentine Mary Pritchett
b. 1 February 1985 (Abbots Morton)
o. Housewife
d. 1969 (Marylebone)

Married Q3 1918

Daisy Ellen Mott
b. 13 June 1883 (Hoddeston)
o. Draper's Assistant
d. 1968 (Devon)

James Ormonde Hudson
b. 6 Jan 1898 (West Bromwich)
o. Company Director
d. 7 March 1981 (Chulmleigh, Devon)

Doris Hambley Parker
b. 27 June 1897 (Co. Galway)
o. Housewife
d. 6 May 1980

Married Q3 1919

Sylvia Mary Price
b. 27 June 1920 (Kings Norton)
o. WAAF then Personal Assistant
d. 6 October 1999 (Lambeth)

Married 6 January 1945
Divorced 1970

Rowland H Hill

Richard Guy Ormonde Hudson
b. 6 September 1920 (Kings Norton)
o. Naval Officer, then Solicitor
d. 26 June 1995 (Chulmleigh, Devon)

Married June 1974

Patricia Jessie Rowland-Hill
b. 28 December 1918 (East Peston)
o. Medical Receptionist
d. 1 December 1994 (Chulmleigh)

Married Q4 1913

Robert Frank Wright
b. 2 August 1919 (Maidstone)
o. Electrician
d. 1992 (Ashford)

Married Q2 1945
Divorced

Richard Guy Ormonde Hudson – Principal Family

The Night Fight

⸺⤜◉◈◉⤛⸺

The briefing room at HMS *Hornet*, the austere Coastal Forces operating base opposite Portsmouth, had been packed with mariners of all hues. Some of this hardened collection of yachtsmen-turned-warriors departed back to the tunnel at Fort Southwick, where the underground Coastal Forces' office resembled an overcrowded railway carriage. Others headed straight for the waterfront pontoons where their majestic Motor Torpedo Boats (MTBs) lay crewed and ready to recommence battle with the Germans. It was the end of the afternoon, the operations team had imparted the plan and another night's work was about to begin. They were as one. Each knew his business and each knew each other's part in mission success.

Two wandering souls needed a lift; their grander hosts were also combat-ready but still at anchor in the Royal Navy's traditional wartime rendezvous, Spithead. They were the Surface Force Direction Officers, known as SFDOs, embarking in the grey-hulled Captain-class Frigates that were to provide radar coverage of the battlefield. The Royal Naval Volunteer Reserve (RNVR) provided most of the wartime manning for Motor Torpedo Boats, and two of their number had developed the very tactics they were about to execute: Temporary Lieutenant Richard Guy Ormonde Hudson RNVR, known to everyone as 'Guy', and Temporary Lieutenant Phillip Gordon Lee DSC (and Bar) RNVR.

The officers of the Coastal Forces were an incestuous navy-within-a-navy. Many knew each other through sustained service in this exclusive sphere of combat, having trusted and relied on each other throughout numerous operations; many owed their lives to their brother officers in other boats. Hudson and Lee were once again going to direct them into combat with the Germans, while ensuring that none accidentally engaged their own side as they careered in packs of three or four boats at 35 knots across the pitch-dark battlefield. The Commanding Officers of the 70-foot Motor Torpedo Boats were only too happy to give their Direction Officers a ride back to work.

A quick telephone call to the Coastal Forces Control Office located in HMS *Dolphin* gained permission to slip moorings and proceed to sea. The night fighters, in their MTBs, were on their way to the French coast, with their Direction Officers tasting the drops of salt spray intruding onto each low-lying MTB's bridge before ascending the steel sides of their control ships.

With the Direction Officers aboard their Frigates, the force steamed through the fading light, heading towards the Eastern maritime flank of the D-Day landings. In the first few days after 6 June 1944 the German navy had been caught unready to repel the invading land forces, but that had now changed. German E-Boats, the nimble equivalent of the British Motor Torpedo Boats, were executing night-fighting excursions from Le Havre, hell-bent on interrupting Allied progress. Hudson and Lee's tactics were keeping them from wreaking havoc.

The Captain-class Frigates, specially designated as control ships, were commanded by regular Navy officers: Lieutenant Commander J S Brown-rigg Royal Navy of HMS *Retalick* and Lieutenant Commander C G H Brown Royal Navy of HMS *Thornborough*. Their mission: to stop enemy E-Boats from attacking the Allies' cross-channel convoys with their German torpedoes, to prevent German minelaying in the Allied assault area, and to stop the Germans from escaping by sea from Le Havre. Their subordinates, massed in Motor Torpedo Boats astern of them, were mainly 'hostilities only' members of the Royal Naval Volunteer Reserve, specially chosen for small ship duty because of some previous connection with the sea. Like Hudson, many had learnt the ways of the sea while sailing in small yachts around the coast of the British Isles. Now, together in wartime formation, they formed the Allies' key maritime barrier protecting the forces liberating Europe.

The force mustered between Cap d'Antifer and Le Havre, on the north coast of France. The control Frigates patrolled along carefully specified lines, between six and eight miles long, dispersed to ensure complete radar coverage. The disposition of the ships was meticulously specified in the Portsmouth Operation Orders for Operation *Neptune*, clearly labelled 'Top Secret' to ensure absolute security from the enemy, while giving enough information to controllers to stop the dreaded fratricide. Their Motor Torpedo Boat attendants made themselves ready to pounce on any detected prey. The recently opened forward operating base at Arromanches then allowed the force to be joined by further locally based MTBs, with especially full fuel tanks.

In the thick darkness of the aspiring battlefield, eyes strained for any sign of enemy activity, aided by the electric wizardry of the radars high on the control ships' masts. As per their orders, each torpedo boat diligently positioned itself in its pre-arranged station. Hudson and Lee's tactics overcame the problem of misidentification by knowing exactly where each boat was held ready to strike, occasionally verified by a radio message telling them to discreetly flash their identity light on a specific bearing towards the control ship's lookout.

Unbeknown to the controllers, the curtain was rising on a final and especially intense period of Coastal Forces action.

The seconds had just ticked past midnight; it was now 24 August 1944. The radar operator in HMS *Thornborough* glimpsed ten new blips on his Plan Position Indicator, a flat radar screen that gave him a God's-eye view of the battlefield. In a drill honed to perfection over the last few weeks, ranges and bearings were passed to the radar plotter, whose paper 'Local Operational Plot', or LOP, yielded the first gem of information: the targets, in a formation one and a half miles off Cap d'Antifer, were steering 060° at a speed of 12 knots. This was exact enemy behaviour.

The LOP officer passed details of the enemy to the SFDO, who verified that they could not be Allied, and who then made his decision to commit the nearest British interceptors. The coder jumbled the SFDO's orders just sufficiently that an enemy overhearing the telegraphist's keystrokes would remain clueless as to their fate, but the intended recipients were able to decode them with rapidity and precision to start their attack. The 'party', as the Coastal Forces called it, was about to begin.

For this attack, the Hunt-class Destroyer HMS *Talybont* would engage from 4,000 yards while MTBs 695 and 692 would attack from the seaward bow. At 15 minutes past midnight *Talybont* opened fire, but the Germans on nearby clifftops responded with illuminating starshell and a hail of gunnery. This was supposed to be a fight, not an attempt at suicide, so the British forces retrograded out of range until a better opportunity arose.

The incestuous SFDOs and their control ship teams had been conspiring; HMS *Retalick* now took over the fight and tracked the ten enemy ships along the coast. The bright light of the German starshell had allowed visual confirmation that the formation included the German Destroyer *V716*, two enemy R-Boat minesweepers, four armed trawlers and two coasters laden with German military supplies. By 0135 they were six miles north

MTBs in transit
SB private collection

of Fécamp, sufficiently offshore to allow a second strike. *Retalick's* SFDO vectored MTBs 212, 208 and 205 to attack with torpedoes, while another Destroyer, HMS *Melbreak*, provided a distraction.

The three MTBs, which had each been trundling at six knots on their 'silent' centreline engine, erupted into a cacophony of exhaust and white water: 'Crash-start wing engines.' Three thousand horsepower was brought online in just a few seconds of exquisitely choreographed engineering drill. Steering the exact vector provided by *Retalick's* SFDO, they closed into 'quarter' formation, sprinting towards their target at 35 knots with only 30 yards between each speeding boat. With darkness punctured by the brilliant flashes of expending gun muzzles they could almost see the whites of their enemy's eyes before they reached the ideal firing position, only 700 yards from their chosen enemy; each fired her volley of two torpedoes in a slight spread to ensure mission success. The MTBs spun onto their disengaging course, their telegraphists instantly reporting this back to the SFDOs; under Hudson and Lee's tactics, such information was crucial to maintain differentiation between friend and foe. Thirty-five seconds later the torpedo boat captains glanced over their shoulders to see the German coaster explode into a hail of shattered metal.

As the MTBs withdrew, HMS *Melbreak* continued the engagement. For 30 minutes she pounded the hapless Germans, sinking the other coaster and seriously damaging both the *V716* and an accompanying trawler. This attack had been a great success, with the vectoring tactics ensuring the two coasters never reached their useful destination, instead taking their cargo to the seabed.

With the arrival of dawn on 24 August the MTBs withdrew to Arromanches to refill their volatile petrol tanks and repair their damage in readiness for the next night of action. Coastal forces policy was that MTBs should not patrol for more than two successive nights, allowing for both repairs and crew rest, but Commanding Officers regularly pleaded with their superiors to override this and get back into the fight – they never wanted to miss a 'party'. The assessment of these superior officers was that the Germans were tonight going to reinforce military units in Le Havre by bringing in supplies from the east, so tonight's patrol areas were moved eastward to allow more time for attacks. It was going to be busy, so the team was reinforced by an additional SFDO, Lieutenant Richard Guy Fison RNVR, and another control ship, HMS *Seymour*. Shortly after darkness, all control ships and their attack forces were in position.

Patrolling six miles northwest of Cap d'Antifer, the coastal forces radar plotter in HMS *Seymour* was the first to gain enemy contact. His display showed four fast-moving blips close to shore. The LOP absorbed each report, and through swift plotting resolved that they were steering 030° at 30 knots – certain enemy behaviour. Hudson and Lee's inter-ship plotting and reporting tactics then came into their own with HMS *Retalick*, stationed off Fécamp, taking over the intercept. She vectored three US Patrol Torpedo (PT) boats towards the enemy and at 2300 battle was joined.

The small US ships started pounding the Germans with their 40- and 37-millimetre guns; the German response was to 'make smoke' and alter course, then increase speed behind this thick acrid screen to evade the traditional visual chase. *Retalick*'s radar was oblivious to the German obfuscation. Continued radar vectoring by her SFDO ensured the Americans remained in contact for the next 15 miles, pummelling and badly damaging the leading German E-Boat. The Germans attempted to distract the SFDO from his precision duties by shelling *Retalick* using their shore-based guns, but the intercept had been a success.

With the battle to their north now in *Retalick*'s safe hands, *Seymour*'s direction team had refocussed on their sector. At 2315, seven miles south of Cap d'Antifer, they detected the first enemy convoy of the night: eight vessels. The SFDO rechecked the disposition of his darkened forces, vectors were passed and MTBs 252, 254, 256 and 257 were ordered to poise for attack. Shortly before the top of the hour they crash-started their wing engines and roared into life. Escorting E-Boats heard their approach and illuminated them in a desperate attempt to stave off the British strike, but minutes after 0100 a wonderful spread of six British torpedoes ejected from their tubes 1,000 yards from the enemy minesweeper *M3857*, which, just under a minute later, exploded spectacularly. The two British Destroyers closed to provide support, volleying 4.7-inch shells into the convoy, setting two E-Boats on fire and damaging a third so badly that the captain of the German *S91* decided to scuttle his small ship.

Working through the hubbub in *Seymour*'s operations room, the coastal forces plotters determined that the convoy had split. Hudson and Lee's tactics were designed to overcome the confusion caused by mixed British and German radar blips diverging on various courses, and Hudson, Lee and Fison conferred by wireless to quickly resolve their plots. They still had fully armed British MTBs available, and they were about to commit them.

MTBs 452, 447 and 453 had lain silently in their patrol lairs; they decoded the vector to two coasters close to Cap d'Antifer, crash-started their wing engines and erupted into high-speed formation to converge on the enemy. They were so close to the beach that the Germans ashore were able to detect them, illuminate them and then engage them with a hail of shrapnel, forcing them to break off this attack when only 900 yards from their target; but, in a wonderful twist of wartime fate, as they eased back into their disengagement formation they ran into two German R-Boat minesweepers. Confirming with their controller that they had located another enemy, they closed into attack formation and engaged from 500 yards; the Germans ashore reopened fire in support of their disaggregated mariners, but it was too late to stop the British MTBs from silencing one enemy R-Boat and setting the other on fire.

The disassembled German convoy remained under the protective umbrella of the shoreside guns between Cap d'Antifer and Fécamp. *Seymour* and *Retalick*'s SFDOs pored over their plots to spot any opportunity to re-engage, but an attempt at 0250 by two MTBs was repelled. Then, on the eastern edge of the screen, five new blips appeared on *Retalick*'s radar. Plotted in an instant, they were only doing four knots headed 260°; were they friend or foe? Plots were resolved and checked, and between them Hudson, Lee and Fison decided to engage. *Retalick* vectored MTBs 205, 209 and 210 from their lair. Six torpedoes were fired at the assessed enemy, and at 0545 a large explosion illuminated the battle-field; in the light of the flash the German Tank Landing Craft *AF103* was seen to be sinking. Precision plotting and surface force direction tactics had again won the engagement.

Daylight delivered a short respite; fuel, ammunition and sleep. Hasty repairs to MTBs were also conjured by the magical engineers of Coastal Forces Mobile Unit 1, led by Commander M H Brind Royal Navy; his MTB base '*en France*' consisted of a series of lorries delivered to the conti-nent a month after the invasion and parked next to improvised berthing trots, which had been towed into position next to one of the sunken ships forming the Arromanches Mulberry harbour. But the three SFDOs remained at sea, Hudson, Lee and Fison tirelessly working with their regular navy Commanding Officers to refine tonight's plan that would continue the blockade of Le Havre.

Under the mask of darkness all the British ships resumed their patrol grids, followed by a few hours of cautious searching. To their west, army stores and supplies continued to flow through the Allied 'spout' into the captured harbours of northern France. A few miles to their east, E-Boats were readying for another desperate night of resistance.

Hudson and Lee's tactics were about to be stretched to their limits. At midnight on 25/26 August it was a shore radar station back in England that gained the first contact. Slick drills, superb wireless telegraphy and, in validation of all the training that had led them to this point, two E-Boats 30 miles to their north were reported to the patrolling force, heading 270° at 30 knots. The Germans were out.

As the enemy attempted to curl around the British Frigates, the radar in HMS *Thornborough* detected them, by now only seven miles off Cap d'An-tifer and closing Le Havre. The SFDOs conferred, and allocated MTBs 481 and 482, under *Thornborough*'s control, to intercept. The E-Boats were the scouting force for a convoy forming up outside Fécamp, and as they retrograded from their British pursuers they led their foe straight into a rich hunting ground. Four hundred yards outside Fécamp lay a flotilla of six enemy Artillery Ferry (AF) barges with more E-Boats protecting them. At 0150 the two British MTBs engaged, setting *AF109* on fire and heavily damaging an E-Boat.

Seizing the opportunity of an enemy thinking he outnumbered his attackers, the SFDOs directed HMS *Thornborough* to close in support, taking a number of direct hits from German artillery, but only as a diversion while their trump card was played; the Free French Navy had also bought into Hudson and Lee's tactics, and FS *La Combattante*, under command of Capitaine de Corvette A Patou DSC FFN, was vectored to approach the convoy. With the Germans distracted by the British attack, the French closed to 3,000 yards before they unleashed hell on their occupiers. By 0245 the French gunners had set two coasters on fire and blown up a third. Their attack continued, with two more coasters sunk and a third forced to beach off Yport. Despite the ongoing mêlée, the SFDOs spotted another opportunity and *Thornborough* vectored MTBs 253, 257 and 255 into the firepit, where they used their six torpedoes to sink an evading R-Boat and a German Tank Landing Craft.

HMS *Seymour* then vectored MTBs under her control to the east of the battle; six German R-Boats, a trawler and a Tank Landing Craft were closing Fécamp under cover of German shore batteries. The hail of German shells from ashore distracted the British from their attack, and, despite the British engaging with both torpedoes and guns, MTBs 773 and 690 were forced to withdraw unsuccessful. US Patrol Torpedo boats then took their cue, closed, fired six torpedoes, but they too were repelled by the firestorm from German shore batteries. No Allies were lost, but the Germans survived to enter Fécamp.

The cycle of daylight recovery and night engagement continued. When night fell on 26 August it was HMS *Retalick*'s direction team that drew first blood. At 0125, patrolling north of Fécamp, the radar detected eight conspicuous blips off Saint-Valery and headed westbound. Hudson and Lee executed their drill; are they friendly? No. Who are the nearest attack units? MTBs 208 and 210. Determine the vector, code it up, transmit, crash-start in the receiving units, and watch the party unfold. At 0150 the two British MTBs made an unobserved attack from 1,000 yards with four torpedoes. Two German Tank Landing Craft were sunk, with the British Commander's report of the battle noting that one 'was apparently carrying ammunition, and blew up and disintegrated'.

The SFDO then vectored HMS *Middleton*, a supporting Destroyer, to close and exploit the confusion of an unalerted attack. *Middleton* scored a series of hits, sinking four or five Tank Landing Craft (such is the uncertainty of night fighting) before the Direction Officer ordered her to cease fire to allow the next wave of torpedo boats to attack. US PTs 520, 511 and 514 attacked with six torpedoes fired from a range of 1,800 yards, scoring another hit. Wave three was then vectored and at 0350 British MTBs 255 and 256 discharged a pattern of four torpedoes, scoring two hits each with very large explosions. The enemy convoy was destroyed. Mission success.

Rest, replan and redeployment took place during the day of 27 August, in preparation for yet another relentless night. By this time each surface force direction team had been in action for nearly 45 nights since D-Day. Men were mentally and physically fatigued. But there was a war on, and an enemy to defeat. The daily tot of rum in every Royal Navy warship probably helped.

At 2340 the direction team in HMS *Thornborough* gained first contact, a small convoy of two coasters and three trawlers being escorted by R-Boats off Cap d'Antifer. MTBs 450, 447 and 482 were vectored to attack with torpedoes, with FS *La Combattante* providing the distraction. At midnight the Free French illuminated the convoy; the clear view of their silhouetted targets allowed the MTBs near-perfect shots and at 0010 two torpedoes struck home, sinking both coasters. As the convoy split into three groups the MTBs reported their disengagement courses and withdrew under the safe cover of Hudson and Lee's identification drill. But the French kept up the attack, scoring hits that set one more ship on fire and damaged yet another.

Two more waves of torpedo attack were vectored, but ten British and US torpedoes failed to elicit any more explosions. The enemy was getting away, with its tail between its legs.

The daily reset routine of the British and American forces took place in an air of anticipation, but the forces sent to patrol on the night of 28 August saw no action. There was no enemy movement. Were they defeated?

The answer came on the night of 29 August 1944, when the Germans attempted to get their last ships out of Fécamp. The Royal Air Force had the night before destroyed the German radar stations at Fécamp and Pointe d'Ailly, reducing the threat from shore batteries, but the extensive German naval minefields remained. Destroyers and control Frigates thus positioned themselves slightly further offshore, with shallow-draught MTBs stationed close to the coast ready to attack.

The party began at 2225 when the direction team in HMS *Retalick* vectored the support Destroyer HMS *Cattistock* to join her and attack an offshore convoy of Tank Landing Craft and a coaster, escorted by R-Boats. At 2235 both ships engaged with gunfire, but the SFDO needed to reclose the coast to maintain the overall plot. *Retalick* reluctantly disengaged just before *Cattistock* was hit by a shell that wrecked her bridge and killed Lieutenant Richard Keddie, her Commanding Officer. Blood was now up. Could they avenge his death?

Retalick tracked the convoy to Dieppe, the SFDO working with his counterpart in HMS *Seymour* to take control of additional MTBs to mass for an attack. But after ten weeks of near-constant operations the small boats were starting to fail. Despite the best efforts of the engineers, one by one they were telegraphing serious material defects and becoming unable to continue a sensible fight. The Germans had been driven from Le Havre and Fécamp, the flanks of the assault area were secure, and there was no justification for further Allied sacrifice; enough lives had already been lost. The night of 29 August marked the last night of Coastal Forces operations off Fécamp and Cap d'Antifer. Job done.

With time to draw breath, the tactics that had so very successfully defended the eastern flank of the landing started to receive universal praise. Coastal Forces had operated in greater numbers than ever before in any one area, demanding exceptional coordination between them and other surface and air forces. The regular navy Commanding Officers of the Destroyers reported that they found the control exercised from the Frigate to be invaluable. In fact, so successful were the surface force direction tactics developed by Hudson and Lee that it was considered 'this development should be exploited and developed for wider spheres of control of ships, particularly in night action.'[1]

Captain Coastal Forces, Captain P V McLaughlin Royal Navy, went on to state that:

> The successful control officers impressed me that as young Lieutenants, RNVR, they possessed a profound technical knowledge and an excellent tactical sense. To Lieutenant P G Lee DSC RNVR, ably seconded by Lieutenant R G O Hudson RNVR, is due a very large measure of the credit for the success and development. They were responsible for the conduct of the early training exercises. By their efficiency they inspired the complete confidence of the Frigate Captains and the MTBs. By their sustained endurance and steady courage in action night after night they showed a fine spirit.[2]

The statistics of the operation are testament to the success of the tactics Hudson and Lee developed. During over 30 actions off the north coast of France there was not a single case of mistaken identity. Thirty-four enemy vessels were sunk, including four E-Boats and seven coasters; two further

---

[1] Report on Operation Overlord – Portsmouth Command (Coastal Forces Enclosure), 765/0/5, 12 September 1944, para. 2.

[2] Report on Operation Overlord – Portsmouth Command (Coastal Forces Enclosure), 765/0/5, 12 September 1944, para. 5.

enemy vessels were driven ashore and 55 enemy vessels were damaged by Allied Coastal Forces operating under the control ship construct. This was at a cost of only seven Allied vessels sunk by enemy E-Boats, including two landing ships, and a further seven Allied vessels damaged by enemy coastal forces.

On 14 November 1944, in a supplement to the *London Gazette*, Temporary Lieutenants Richard Guy Ormonde Hudson and Richard Guy Fison RNVR were each awarded the Distinguished Service Cross, and Temporary Lieutenant Phillip Gordon Lee RNVR was awarded a second bar to his DSC. The citation is simple:

> For outstanding enterprise and skill in preventing the enemy from bringing supplies to and withdrawing troops from Le Havre.[3]

Guy Hudson would wear his DSC with pride for the rest of his life, despite the hell he had endured while earning it.

---

[3] Fourth supplement to the *London Gazette* of 10 November 1944, dated 14 November 1944, p.5226.

Making the Man

—◦◉◦—

On 6 September 1920 a baby boy was born in Kings Norton, Birmingham, to James and Doris Hudson. James was 22 years old and worked for his father in 'the Hudson Studios Ltd'. He had married the year before, after his sweetheart moved to Birmingham from County Galway, where James' father had grown up prior to emigrating to the industrial midlands of England.

The baby was christened Richard Guy Ormonde Hudson. 'Richard' was chosen in tribute to his grandfather, who had built the photography and fine art business that now provided his parents' income, as well as his great-grandfather, and also his great-great-grandfather, who had served under Wellington at the Battle of Waterloo; it was a longstanding family name. 'Ormonde' was a middle name shared with his father and reflected the family's Irish roots in the former Dukedom of Ormonde. And 'Guy', well, that middle name went on to become the young boy's moniker.

James Hudson had married Doris Hambley Parker in the summer of 1919 and Richard Guy Ormonde Hudson, or Guy (as this book will hereafter refer to him), was their first and only child. He was brought up in a pleasant new home at 100 Middleton Hall Road, Warwickshire, close to his grandparents' rather larger residence just down the lane at Middleton Hall farmhouse near the new Kings Norton station. Theirs was a close-knit family, and Guy was loved by his four aunties as well as his paternal grandparents; James was their only son, a 'middle' child who had three older sisters, Kathleen, Harriet and Marjorie, plus Barbara, his younger sister, who all still lived with their father.

Guy's grandfather, Richard Henry Hudson, had made a great deal of money through his very successful photography business. Born in 1860 in Galway, Ireland, Richard had travelled aged 21 to West Bromwich, near Birmingham, where he lived in a boarding house at 142 Soho Hill. He soon met Annie Matilda Mary Sunderland, who was five years his junior. Annie was the daughter of James Sunderland, who was one of the first photographers in the area. James Sunderland had started his own small photographic business, training Annie to assist him as his 'photographic colourist'. With headquarters in the Grand Western Arcade, Birmingham, within a few years the 'J Sunderland Special Studio for Large Portraits' had expanded to include four further shops in Sheffield (6 Norfolk Row), Dudley (2 Stafford Street), Wolverhampton (53 Queen Street) and Leamington (45 Bath Street).

Richard Hudson and Annie Sunderland had married on 20 May 1884 in West Bromwich. Richard was then made a partner in his father-in-law's business, which was renamed 'Sunderland and Hudson: Special Studio for Large Portraits'. The new management team consolidated the business to four studios, keeping their headquarters in Birmingham's Great Western Arcade, moving the Dudley studio to 220 Market Place, acquiring new studios in Wolverhampton (96 Darlington Street) and Walsall (7 High Street), and moving out of Leamington and Sheffield. Further rebranding and the semi-retirement of Annie's father dropped the original 'Sunderland' and saw the name adjusted to 'Hudson and Co'.[4] The successful photography business was now firmly under the Hudson family.

As Grandfather Richard became older, the running of the business was increasingly taken on by his son James. However, James was less adept as a businessman than Richard Hudson, spending the family fortune faster than it was being replenished. Notwithstanding James' lack of business acumen, Guy lived a comfortable life, which included good schooling and regular trips to see relatives. His mother's family were still in Ireland, and Guy travelled often to visit them during holidays.

---

[4] This must not be confused with another Birmingham company of the same name, founded in 1870 by Joseph Hudson, which made whistles.

The family business — SB private collection

Guy Hudson learning to sail with James and Doris Hudson — SB private collection

Living far from the ocean near landlocked Birmingham, it was during these trips to Galway that Guy first developed his love of the sea, learning to sail in small open boats around the rocky Irish coast. He was a quiet child, and these were small adventures that distracted him from life near an industrial English city. However, he eventually found many of these family holidays boring and he was often lonely with few people to play with. He was also forced to travel to Switzerland; his doctor had diagnosed a 'shadow' on his lung for which the fresh air at a clinic in the Alps was deemed beneficial, and Guy was thus taken for a few months' respite on the continent before returning to Birmingham and resuming his studies.

By 1926 Grandfather Richard was 66. He had been maintaining a second home in Seaton on the South Devon coast where his younger mistress, Margaret Leigh, lived with his other son, who was also called Richard but did not share his surname. Working with his family lawyer, Mr Hubert Davenport Price MC, to achieve an amicable split, he had left his wife and daughters in the decaying Middleton Hall farmhouse and moved in with Margaret, also taking from Birmingham his cook, Alice Claridge, who was to remain with him for the rest of his life.

Guy became a regular visitor to his grandfather at Seaton, enjoying the countryside and developing a love for life in Devon, while his grandfather enjoyed the financial fruits of his business success. It was about this time that Grandfather Richard introduced Guy to the sedate lawn sport of croquet, including a Hudson family custom of having a trolley of drinks at each end of the court. The favoured Hudson family refreshment appears to have been a rather strong version of gin and tonic, although history does not reveal if this helped or hindered the malleting accuracy of those who consumed it.

By April 1934 the family income was diminishing as the photographic trade became more competitive, but it still allowed Guy to be enrolled at Rugby School in Warwickshire, boarding in School House. Rugby School was, and still is, a quintessential English public school. Attended by the children of those who can afford the relatively substantial fees, it was immortalised in the popular 1857 novel *Tom Brown's School Days*, written by Old Rugbeian (former pupil) Thomas Hughes. Guy's school had given its name to the now global sport of rugby, which has its roots on the school playing fields when in 1823 William Webb Ellis demonstrated his total disregard for the rules of football by taking the ball in his arms and running with it.

Guy maintained his quiet persona while at Rugby School, restricting his sporting endeavours to minor participation in hockey, tennis and squash, despite the reputation of his academic host. He was a very bright student whose passions became science and ornithology, through which he was an especially active member of the school natural history society. Unsurprisingly, he used his family pictorial expertise to excel in the photographic section of the society, but he also became especially adept at understanding the avian populations in the area near the school.

In 1938 he was appointed as Honorary Secretary of the school ornithology society, managing the membership of five masters and 32 pupils. He then wrote a superb and very detailed piece for the society's annual report titled 'The Birds of Rugby District', listing his many personal sightings of a wide variety of bird life as well as exploiting many years of detailed records scripted by his fellow twitchers. This work was so meticulous and of such academic significance that he was later cited by the author David Ballance in his book *Birds in Counties: An Ornithological Bibliography of the Counties of England, Wales, Scotland and the Isle of Man* (London: Imperial College Press, 2000). Guy's article also showed his attention to detail by including a cautious dressing-down for his compatriots: 'It must be impressed that ringing is of little or no use unless results are absolutely accurate. One or two ringers have made errors this year, and these go some way to mar admirable work by the majority.' This article won him a school prize for his 'distinguished work'.

Academically Guy did well at school, relaxing by either birdwatching or fishing, especially at the nearby Fawsley Park. A pinnacle of this extracurricular school life occurred in 1939, when he was awarded the school's

Guy Hudson (right) — SB private collection

Stanford Prize for Ornithology, receiving a postal order for the princely sum of £2.

He had also joined the school's Officer Training Corps, where his field skills and military acumen earned him 'Certificate A: Infantry'. In the run-up to possible war, this was a significant achievement as it granted the holder eligibility for consideration for a commission in the Supplementary Reserve or the Territorial Army, together with exemption from certain elements of training. Dated 8 March 1938, just over a year before the outbreak of World War II, it also instructed the holder that 'In the event of a national emergency involving mobilization of the Regular Army and embodiment of the Territorial Army, he is requested to notify his address to [the War Office] with any offer of service he may wish to make.'

Guy finished his formal schooling in the summer of 1938. Conflict on the continent of Europe already appeared possible, and as the holidays approached he sat through a tender but prescient end-of-term speech by Percy Lyon, the headmaster:

> Whatever may come of our present discontents, whether the storm breaks or floats away, there will be need in the world in ten or twenty years hence of fresh efforts by a new generation to build on a surer basis . . . The eternal ideals remain: truth, love, justice, sympathy and loyalty. They do not perish because men are false to them. They will return again when we have again become worthy to entertain them.[5]

Guy remained at Rugby for the traditional 'Upper Sixth' additional term reserved for those headed for Oxbridge. During Michaelmas term 1938, Guy's last, the school ramped up its preparations for war. Pupils were formed into digging parties engaged in creating trenches in which to shelter from air raids, and in early October gas masks were distributed to all pupils.

Guy finally departed in December 1938, filling the few months between school and university preparing himself for a career in his chosen field of law. He had matured into a man of 5 foot 10 inches, with gentle blue eyes and a fresh complexion. He was ready to move into the wide world beyond home and school. He travelled for a period, ending up once more in Switzerland, where he spent time with his grandfather, Richard, and Richard's partner Margaret. Tragically, on 8 August 1939, Margaret passed away, leaving Grandfather Richard with a huge hole in his life and Guy with simple memories of a wonderful friend, just before many more lives were to be extinguished on the same continent.

On 3 September 1939 the crisis in Europe resulted in the United Kingdom declaring war on Germany. Six weeks later, on 17 October 1939, Guy matriculated into the University of Oxford, attending St John's College to read jurisprudence. He was still surrounded by friends, with fellow School House pupil H W S Montefiore also matriculating as a

---

[5] *The Meteor* (magazine of Rugby School), 8 July 1938, p. 86.

first-year into St John's College, and M D Spencer, also of School House, at St John's as a second-year undergraduate. They were overseen by Old Rugbeian E L B Meurig-Davies, who by that time was a lecturer in classics at their new college. And across the whole university there were a further 37 Old Rugbeians starting their first year — enough from one school to field two full rugby teams, with replacements!

Guy promptly joined the University of Oxford Officer Training Corps, where he combined his legal studies with further military training, gaining his 'Certificate B: Artillery'. He also passed his first series of academic exams, satisfying the moderators in December that he had mastered Roman Law, going on during Hilary term to pass his moderations in Criminal Law, Constitutional Law and Legal History. But by now he was becoming distracted by the fighting in Europe and considerations of how he could best serve his country.

Over the summer of 1940 Guy decided to follow the advice on his school infantry certificate, but instead of remaining on land he resolved to follow his love of the sea. On 19 August 1940 he requested to join the Royal Naval Volunteer Reserve. Under wartime recruitment procedures, volunteers for naval service generally received their first choice, if they were fit enough. Guy was, and as an experienced yachtsman who held an Officer Training Corps certificate, he pursued his eligibility for consideration for commission. But under the Royal Navy system of selection he would first have to serve as a rating to prove his ability to lead and to inspire. He rapidly received confirmation of his call-up and on 11 September 1940 he reported to HMS *Royal Arthur*, the new entry training establishment of the Royal Navy's Chatham port division.

Serving His Country

———◦◎◦———

Guy Hudson joined the Royal Navy on 11 September 1940, being allocated the service number JX220481 as a seaman enrolling under a hostilities-only engagement.

It was one week after his 20th birthday that he walked through the entrance of HMS *Royal Arthur*, a former Butlins holiday camp at Ingoldmells, near Skegness, that had been taken over by the Ministry of War under the Naval Mobilisation Act of 1938. It was a rather lovely place to start his naval service, opened by the entrepreneur Billy Butlin only three years earlier. Butlin had built it as an ideal family retreat. It still had a cinema, a theatre, tennis courts and playing fields, all intended to entertain holidaymakers but now used to indoctrinate more urgently needed warfighters. And the swimming pool had been put to rather more pragmatic use than the designer's family-centric intent through the military application of a few coats of drab paint and the launching of a 27-foot Royal Navy rowing whaler onto its glistening surface.

Guy was accommodated in one of the chalets, sharing his 'cabin' (as named by the Royal Navy) with three other new entrants. Once he was issued with his new uniform, daily instruction focussed on basic naval discipline as well as trade training. With over 2,000 people in the establishment, HMS *Royal Arthur* trained sailors across a plethora of trades, but the exigencies of wartime meant that each individual sailor was taught only the basics of his specific job before being despatched to the fleet.

Already identified as a candidate for commission, Guy was assigned to one of the shorter training courses which qualified him as a 'coder', ready to join the front line for six months of assessment for potential

Ordinary Seaman Hudson (left) with 'Maurice, Mike and John'
SB private collection

officer training, as well as providing vital manpower for the maritime battle against Germany. Using some of the exemptions provided by his Officer Training Corps service, he spent only five weeks at HMS *Royal Arthur* before he was assigned to the Chatham Division barracks at HMS *Pembroke*.

Now rated as an Ordinary Seaman, he had to wait two months for his first ship. Conditions in the barracks were markedly less salubrious than the holiday camp in which he had first experienced regular naval life. However, he did have Christmas ashore before being sent off with three fellow officer candidates to join his first seagoing unit.

On 30 December 1940 Guy embarked in HMS *Sikh*, a Tribal-class Destroyer built in Glasgow and commissioned in 1939. A member of the 4th Destroyer Flotilla, she was employed on screening operations escorting convoys and protecting the Royal Navy's capital ships from marauding German U-Boats or other patrolling enemy ships. For this mission, HMS *Sikh* was later awarded the battle honour 'Atlantic 1940–41'.

HMS Sikh — Medway Studios

Guy's new home was a nimble escort built around a main armament of eight 4.7-inch guns on four 'twin' mountings, four 21-inch torpedo tubes which could be rotated to fire either to port or to starboard, and 20 depth charges. Displacing around 2,500 tons when fully armed, the Tribal class had two extremely powerful steam turbines which could drive them at up to 36 knots during close combat. HMS *Sikh* was also a crowded ship, with 190 ship's company to man all her weapons as well as the relatively new ASDIC anti-submarine sensor. In such a small space, everyone knew everyone.

Only seven days after joining his new ship, Guy witnessed one of the hazards of life at sea. On 6 January 1941 HMS *Mashona*, a fellow Tribal-class Destroyer, collided with the starboard quarter of HMS *Sikh,* causing considerable damage. From January to March 1941 HMS *Sikh* underwent repairs and modifications in the Henry Robb shipyard, Leith, Scotland, where the opportunity was taken to fit her with a modified Royal Air Force air–surface radar known as Type 286M. Radar at the time was still in its operational infancy, and this type of radar had an aerial which was fixed to the ship's structures and therefore was of limited operational use while underway. Guy was thus on a ship at the forefront of maritime radar use, and may at this time have started to develop the understanding of this new technology that was to mark his later naval career as a tactical pioneer of radar control for Motor Torpedo Boats. Guy would also at this time have been introduced to the Royal Navy tradition of 'up spirits', or the daily tot of rum; this was not served in shore establishments, but on a warship a daily dose of alcohol was seen as vital to steady both nerve and stomach.

HMS Mashona, pictured by Able Seaman Hudson from on board HMS Sikh, 6 January 1941 — SB private collection

After a short period of working up, *Sikh* operated out of the fleet anchorage at Scapa Flow, including on 18 April 1941 being tasked on a search and rescue operation in the North Sea. General escort duties followed, but no actions of significance occurred in Guy's first few months of life at sea. But this was soon to change.

On 21 May 1941 HMS *Sikh*, in company with HM Ships *Cossack*, *Maori* and *Zulu*, left the river Clyde for a convoy escort of troops transiting the Western Approaches. During their passage to meet the convoy they were diverted and ordered to bolster a protective screen of ships around the battleship HMS *King George V*, which had been despatched to sink the German battleship *Bismarck*.

Sinking the German raider was a very high priority for the British Admiralty. *Bismarck* was one of the best-armed and best-armoured German warships ever built, and the thought of having her loose in the Atlantic filled both politicians and Allied sailors with dread. She needed to break out of the North Sea and into the deep ocean to be able to fulfil her destructive role, so the Royal Navy despatched ships to all potential transit routes with the sole intent of sinking her.

On 24 May, as she transited through the Denmark Strait, *Bismarck* was intercepted by the 22-year-old British battleship HMS *Hood*. As battle was joined, each fired volleys of their destructive shells, desperately hoping to penetrate the other's armour plating and disable her foe. The 15-inch guns of HMS *Hood* should have been a fairly even match for the 15-inch guns in *Bismarck*, but within a few minutes of the start of the engagement, at a range of just over 18,000 yards, either superior German gunnery or a very lucky shot saw a German shell penetrate *Hood*'s 12-inch armour and detonate inside her. *Hood* erupted in a catastrophic internal explosion, killing all but three of her complement. 1,418 British sailors were killed.

This news reached HMS *Sikh*, whose ship's company were downcast at this apparent defeat. In the increasingly rough weather it appeared that *Bismarck* had escaped. The British did not, however, give up, and waves of aircraft were sent to search for her.

At 1100 on 26 May an aircraft sighted *Bismarck* 70 miles from HMS *Sikh*, steaming south at 24 knots. *Sikh* altered course to close with her, increasing speed to 28 knots and rolling 30 to 40 degrees in the very rough weather. During the afternoon a sailor was washed overboard, and despite the treacherous conditions a rapid turn was made in order to recover him. Superb ship handling saw *Sikh* close to within 15 yards of the man in the water, but, despite safety being so very close, the sea overcame him just before the moment of rescue and he slipped beneath the foaming waves. Many of Guy's fellow ship's company witnessed their shipmate's demise, but the enemy still beckoned and there was no time for them to mourn.

Heavy rain squalls were obscuring an effective lookout, but at 2220

Bismarck was sighted about 18,000 yards ahead. Along with her fellow Tribal-class Destroyers, *Sikh* edged closer to her prey, tightening the net despite an occasional speculative shell from the evading German battleship. Keen to maintain contact and report her position to the pursuing British battle fleet, *Sikh* used the mask of darkness to close to within 7,000 yards, Guy and his fellow coders working tirelessly to ensure their supporting warships knew everything that their enemy attempted. Then, just after midnight, *Bismarck* turned broadside to *Sikh* and let loose her entire main armament.

The first shells landed just 30 yards from *Sikh*, who increased to full speed, turned hard about and made smoke. With towering columns of water being thrown up by every new salvo, the situation was desperate as *Sikh* sought sanctuary either out of range or obscured by her thick smoke. After enduring a full five salvos from the German battleship, *Sikh* managed to evade unscathed. 4.7-inch Destroyer shells were useless against such a well-armoured foe, so *Sikh* stood off as a distraction, reporting the enemy while *Cossack*, *Maori* and *Zulu* closed to attack with torpedoes; they assessed either two or three hits between them, but the enemy was only wounded.

Just after 0200 on 27 May *Sikh* turned about and closed to make her attack. She loosed her four torpedoes directly at the enemy's damaged hull before beating a hasty retreat; one torpedo struck home, but the hardy German battleship again survived. The four 'Tribals' then formed up in a tracking formation around the limping enemy to maintain reports to the pursuing British battleships.

The darkness, rough sea and squally weather were hindering almost any form of visual tracking and contact became intermittent. Just before dawn, in order to prevent his ship being silhouetted against the morning light, *Sikh*'s Commanding Officer, Commander Graham Stokes Royal Navy, positioned his ship to the west of where he believed *Bismarck* to be hobbling along. As eyes were trying to adjust to the increased visibility offered by the peeking sun at 0625, HMS *Maori* fired a starshell to illuminate what her lookouts believed was the German raider. On board HMS *Sikh* the starboard lookout then saw *Bismarck* emerge from a rain squall barely 7,000 yards away. The First Lieutenant, David Cole-Hamilton, yelled for the captain to turn away, and the ship beat a hasty retreat. It appears that lookouts in *Bismarck* were having as much difficulty observing their enemy as were the British, and no German shells were unleashed.

At 0845, two British battleships arrived to finish the job. HMS *Rodney* opened fire at 0847, followed a minute later by HMS *King George V*. After a short artillery duel in which the battered *Bismarck* bravely defended her honour, the British battle fleet confirmed their maritime superiority by pulping the German into a smoking wreck.

At 1010 HMS *Norfolk* closed the German derelict and unleashed four torpedoes at the now wallowing hulk, scoring two possible hits. HMS *Dorsetshire* then closed to 3,600 yards, fired two torpedoes and saw them both explode under the floundering German. At 1036, HMS *Dorsetshire* curled around the bow of *Bismarck,* fired another torpedo from 2,600 yards into her port side, and saw the great German battleship heel over quickly to port and commence to sink by the stern. Just before 1040 her bow cocked upwards, and with a nod to King Neptune *Bismarck* slid from sight.

HMS *Dorsetshire* immediately began to recover survivors from the 2,300 German crew who had been on board. Rolling in the steep sea, rafts, buoys, hawsers and life lines were thrown over the side and about 80 men were soon on board, plucked from near-certain death in the freezing waters. HMS *Maori* joined her, recovering from the water a further 30 men, before 'a suspicious smokey discharge was observed about 2 miles away'.[6] Rescue efforts immediately ceased.

At 1100, closing from their ringside seat to the position of the watery grave, those on board *Sikh* had to endure steaming through a sea of detritus from a deceased battleship. Although some German sailors remained in

---

6 BR 1736 (3/50): The Chase and Sinking of the *Bismarck*. Naval Staff History, Second World
   War, Battle Summary No. 5, p. 34.

the water, the suspected presence of a German U-Boat now prohibited further British attempts to pick them up. From his position near the bridge, Guy saw some of these men in the water, men of his own age and with faces and complexions similar to his. But war was hell and winning required your own survival. Under orders not to pick up survivors, *Sikh* turned away to fight another day, and Guy started his attempts to erase that particular memory.

Only another five Germans were recovered alive; three were rescued that evening by the German submarine *U-74*, who had been the cause of the British angst during their own rescue mission, and two more were recovered the following day by the German fishing vessel *Sachenwald,* who had been operating as a weather ship from Bordeaux. Thereafter the Spanish cruiser *Canarias* arrived on the scene to find nothing more than floating bodies.

For her part in the destruction of this enemy, HMS *Sikh* was awarded the battle honour 'Bismarck Action 1941'.

Only a week later, on 3 June 1941, HMS *Sikh* joined convoy WS9A, which she escorted for four days in the North-West Approaches prior to returning to the Clyde. Sailing in time to meet the aircraft carrier HMS *Victorious*, she then acted as part of the carrier's escort as far as Gibraltar prior to HMS *Victorious* delivering her aircraft to Malta under the banner of Operation *Tracer*.

Having tasted the entrance to the Mediterranean, from Gibraltar *Sikh* this time returned to Plymouth, where on 16 June 1941 Guy disembarked for a four-week break before commencing his training as an officer.

HMS *King Alfred* was the designated training establishment for Royal Naval Volunteer Reserve officers. A reportedly daunting place, it required officer candidates (known as cadets) to develop their 'officer-like qualities', known as OLQs, as well as master a busy curriculum of naval subjects required to deliver victory in maritime combat.

Prior to the war, *King Alfred* was the designation of the Motor Launch (ML 1649) attached to the Sussex division of the Royal Naval Volunteer

Reserve. On the outbreak of war the Royal Navy determined that it needed a site at which to start training significant numbers of new officers, and a new 'Marina Complex' with swimming baths and leisure centre near the Sussex RNVR Division was chosen and requisitioned. It was commissioned HMS *King Alfred* on 11 September 1939, under the command of Captain John Pelly CBE, Royal Navy.

Training there initially focussed on the mobilisation of the Royal Naval Volunteer (Supplementary) Reserve, which had been formed in 1936 for men between the ages of 18 and 39 who were interested in yachting or similar pursuits. The course was duly designed around those who were familiar with the maritime but needed militarisation. Once the cohort of RNV(S)R had been mobilised, an extended course was required to allow recruitment from a wider pool of the population, who needed both marinisation and militarisation.

In early 1940, in order to create space for this additional training requirement, HMS *King Alfred* was extended over three sites. At Hove on the south coast of England was the former Mowden School, which had been evacuated to Market Harborough in Northamptonshire in order to enhance protection for the pupils, thereby freeing the buildings. This was requisitioned and designated HMS *King Alfred* (M). Another nearby school, Lancing College, had also been evacuated (this time to Shropshire), and was upon requisition designated HMS *King Alfred* (L). A three-phase, ten-week course was then created with two weeks at Mowden, six weeks at Lancing, and the final two weeks at the original leisure centre base.

On 18 July 1941 Guy reported to his second wartime holiday camp. But the next ten weeks were to be anything but a holiday. Along with his fellow officer candidates he was drilled in the minutiae of seamanship and navigation required to be an effective officer in the Royal Navy's small coastal craft. The wastage rate on the course was up to 33 per cent, so it was far from a foregone conclusion that Cadet Rating Hudson (of Drake Division) would pass, and he had to study diligently to pass all the required exams and earn the right to change from his seaman's uniform into that of an officer. His studies included 'Power of Command', 'Coastal Navigation', 'Pilotage' (handling a ship in the confines of a harbour), 'Naval Signalling', 'Practical Seamanship', 'Gunnery', and 'Torpedoes and Mines'.

Guy was also introduced to the naval sextant, which required precision and skill to manipulate. It was used to measure the exact angles of the stars needed to 'fix' a ship's position by applying an understanding of astronomy. The operator would need to find and learn the names of some of heaven's brightest stars, such as Castor and Pollux.

He was successful, passing his course and earning two rewards. The first was a commission into the Royal Naval Volunteer Reserve as a Temporary Sub-Lieutenant, dated 25 September 1941. The second was a £40 grant from the government with which to go and buy his new uniform!

Guy Hudson (front right) as a newly commissioned officer — SB private collection

Guy stayed on the books on HMS *King Alfred* for a further month before being despatched to the Royal Navy school of gunnery at HMS *Excellent*, where he would start his specialist training. From 27 October 1941 he spent one week learning the art and science of engaging the enemy with naval guns, qualifying as a small ship's gunnery officer, before he was despatched to the cold of Scotland.

Commissioned in October 1940, HMS *St Christopher* was the wartime training base for the Royal Navy's Coastal Forces. With its shore headquarters in the Highland Hotel, Fort William, the scenery of the Scottish Highlands made a truly spectacular backdrop for the completion of Guy's specialist training.

HMS *St Christopher* ran various courses associated with Coastal Forces operations and Motor Torpedo Boats. Each lasted only a few weeks prior to students being moved along towards front line duty. As well as extensive shiphandling and formation manoeuvres, the Motor Torpedo Boat course included the firing of two practice torpedoes from two separate MTBs prior to certification.

On 3 November 1941 Guy commenced the five weeks of theory and practical instruction required to make him into a true Coastal Forces warrior. Successfully proving his ability to lead, direct and engage, on 15 December he was assigned to Motor Torpedo Boat 233 for his seagoing certifications. The next weeks saw him achieve underway gunnery, navigation and torpedo firings in the relative safety of Scottish lochs.

Upon completion of his training, which he passed with flying colours, he was assessed as having the highest possible 'personal qualities'. His professional ability and ship handling ability were rated as 'good' and he earned a recommendation that in due course he should be considered for sea command.

With this glowing report under his belt, he proceeded south to the Coastal Forces base in HMS *Hornet*, where he would join his first operational MTB.

His Majesty's Motor Torpedo Boat 62 was a 70-foot MTB built by Vospers. She had been ordered in 1939 as part of a 'war programme' purchase of 34 boats. Eight of these, MTBs 57 to 65, were commissioned between October 1941 and March 1942, with a decision in December 1941 that this batch was to be sent to Alexandria, in the Mediterranean, to form the 7th MTB Flotilla.

The 70-foot MTBs had a ship's company of ten. They were usually commanded by a Lieutenant (often in the Royal Naval Volunteer Reserve) with a Sub-Lieutenant as their Executive Officer, or First Lieutenant, who was also the ship's navigator. The Commanding Officer, or CO, ran and fought the ship from the open-topped bridge, whilst the First Lieutenant ran the operational plot in the enclosed steering position just below and forward of the captain's station. The First Lieutenant also had a roving role about the upper deck supervising the seaman-torpedo rating who managed and fired the main armament of two 21-inch heavyweight torpedoes, as well as the deck gunner.

The torpedoes were very similar to those launched from submarines, fired forward from their tubes on whichever course the MTB was on when they were released. They would be loaded in harbour by pushing them into the two torpedo tubes (one each side of the bridge), and were ejected either by the Commanding Officer pulling the discharge handles on the bridge, or by a local firing handle at the back of each tube. These local handles were an essential secondary method of firing, as many Motor Torpedo Boats suffered damage to the bridge firing mechanisms from enemy gunfire while speeding at about 25 knots towards their targets. The ideal torpedo firing range was about 700 yards. The sound of the 'pop' from the 15-ounce cordite impulse explosive charge that drove the torpedoes out of their tubes was always a very welcome interruption to the cacophony of battle, as it meant that the MTB could at last turn away from the enemy, its explosive payload now on an uninterruptible course towards its often still firing foe.

Returning the enemy's gunfire was achieved from the deck-mounted gun.

MTB 62 was fitted with one twin (i.e. two-barrelled) 0.5-inch machine gun, in the centre of the after deck. This was manned by a rating gunner who was responsible for all aspects of maintaining, ammunitioning, aiming and firing it. Also working on deck, if sufficient manpower was available, were two other seaman ratings who assisted with the local firing of torpedoes and also the dropping of depth charges off the stern of the boat. An especially daring tactic required the MTB to cross the bow of the enemy as close as they could (usually 20 to 30 yards) and roll two depth charges (of the four carried) into their target's path, such that the depth charges slowly sank as the enemy steamed over them, to blow up directly under the centre of the enemy's keel (resulting in what is called 'breaking the enemy's back'). The upper deck team also operated smoke generators at the stern of the boat, which could create a thick, opaque and toxic screen behind the manoeuvring MTB and inside which a well-handled boat could hide.

Getting into a firing position for either torpedoes or depth charges relied on three petrol Hall-Scott V12 engines, which could generate a total of 1,800 brake horsepower (BHP) and drive the 40-ton boats at a speed of up to 25 knots. The original design for 70-foot MTBs had used Italian-made Isotta Fraschini petrol engines which had generated twice the total power and had given a top speed of 40 knots, but the entry of Italy into the war as an enemy had stopped the supply of these more powerful units. One of the engines, on the centreline, was especially well insulated for sound and was used as the 'silent running' propulsion unit when lying in wait for a target. The other two could be crash-started in only a few seconds by the motor mechanic in charge of the engine room, and his two stoker assistants; they did not 'stoke' the engines, but the Royal Navy had retained this nomenclature from the days of coal by way of recognising the vital role of such hard-working men, who endured very hot and extremely cramped working conditions.

MTB 62 was a generally good example of potentially superb British shipbuilding. The design was simple and could be fabricated by any number of small boatyards that could create the wooden structural sections. These were bolted together before being encased in a planked wooden hull. The bow had a reinforced forepeak which could be used to store some items, but which was also a sacrificial section of the vessel encapsulated by a watertight bulkhead to protect the rest of the boat from flooding if an enemy ship had to be rammed. The crew's quarters were aft of this bulkhead, with sufficient beds for everyone to sleep on board if required, although the area was mainly used for eating meals or intermittent rest between warfighting engagements.

Moving aft, an enclosed wheelhouse and operational plotting area was built onto the otherwise smooth upper deck. As well as space for charts, code books and operational plans, this area housed some radios and wireless direction-finding equipment used to intercept enemy radio transmissions. The aft end of the wheelhouse had a short ladder of four steps which led up to the open bridge, which had a steering position and throttles as well as the flag locker to hoist visual signals to other boats in company. And below the enclosed wheelhouse were the very cramped wireless telegraphy office and officers' wardroom.

On the upper deck either side of the bridge were the torpedo tubes, 23 feet long and 21 inches in diameter, which were the main armament of any Motor Torpedo Boat. Each tube was angled slightly outwards, away from the centreline, by eight and a half degrees, with each torpedo pre-set with a 'gyro angle' of eight degrees such that on firing they would turn eight degrees back towards the bow of the MTB, leaving the torpedoes diverging at an angle of one degree when ejected in the usual 'salvo' of a twin firing.

Between the rearmost ends of the torpedo tubes, where the 'local' torpedo firing positions were manned, was the aft gun mounting, surrounded by a protective metal sheath designed to keep the gunner alive even when faced with returning enemy fire. But underneath the gun (and gunner) was the main fuel tank, containing up to 2,000 gallons of petrol. Immediately aft of this fuel tank was the engine room and associated three drive shafts, which took up nearly one third of MTB 62's length. And in the last six feet of her hull was another pair of fuel tanks, intertwined (or so it often felt) with the steering gear.

Guy arrived at HMS *Hornet* on 19 January 1942. His new Commanding Officer, Lieutenant Clive Finch RNVR, was already on board, and MTB 62 quickly sailed for a series of local sea trials prior to departing, on 9 February 1942, for passage from Portsmouth headed to the Clyde. As the junior of only two officers on board, Guy was the new First Lieutenant and Second-in-Command.

This was a long passage for a small craft with a small crew and limited accommodation, but it was swiftly accomplished. Six days later the delivery voyage had been completed and Guy, under the temporary administrative command of HMS *Nile* (the Royal Navy's eastern Mediterranean administrative base in Alexandria), was despatched with the rest of MTB 62's crew on a troopship headed for Egypt; he left Great Britain on 15 February 1942, not to return for over a year.

WARM WATERS —
HOT ENGAGEMENTS

———⋅∾⊙∾⋅———

MTB 62 had lain in Glasgow for nearly a month waiting for a cargo ship that could carry her. On 20 March 1942 she was hoisted on board SS *Barrister*, which sailed five days later for the extremely long passage to Alexandria.

Due to the presence of German forces off the French coast and throughout the Mediterranean, especially German bomber and torpedo aircraft, *Barrister* took a very offshore route south through the Atlantic, around the Cape of Good Hope, and then north along the African coast towards the Red Sea. The weather in the South Atlantic was terrible, with MTB 62, in her upper-deck cradle, suffering some storm damage. *Barrister* transited Suez on 3 June 1942, and within a few days she offloaded her valuable cargo into the warm waters off HMS *Mosquito*, the eastern Mediterranean Coastal Forces base that was by now Guy's home.

The 7th MTB Flotilla had formed under the overall command of Lieutenant Robert A M Hennessy RNVR. Due to his boats having been delivered in Portsmouth in a piecemeal, staggered fashion they had not worked up as a team. This meant that taking them into battle was at best risky, and at worst could see his force decimated. Guy's boat, along with most of the others, also needed to be repaired as their steering gear was proving to be especially fragile. Thus, the 7th MTB Flotilla started to spend considerable periods alongside, with no action.

An officer's life in Alexandria was an interesting change from Guy's earlier naval experiences. The headquarters of the admiral's staff were located ashore at HMS *Nile* in King Farouk's palace at Ras el-Tin. HMS *Mosquito* was an 'independent' command established at the adjacent Mahroussa Jetty, where the Coastal Forces could aggregate, repair and prepare for operations. The Coastal Forces had by this stage in the war established quite a reputation for themselves as ferocious in combat but also ruthlessly efficient at socialising. Compared with rum for the lower deck, gin and tonic was often the tipple of choice, and, with their MTBs unavailable for operations, Guy and his fellow MTB officers of the 7th Flotilla would have been able to make the most of the opportunities to build their camaraderie.

Social invitations between MTBs were common, and the ethos of the Coastal Forces command demanded regular exchanges of operational information to optimise tactics against an enemy who were adept at morphing their procedures almost as fast as the Royal Navy. The Coastal Forces command was by this time publishing a regular bulletin of recent actions, known as the *Coastal Forces Periodic Review*, which also contained tactical notices and engineering feedback. As well as disseminating information, this publication was intended to promote discussions among MTB officers of innovative methods of defeating the enemy. Such discussions were often fuelled by alcohol and were almost indistinguishable from social events, with the common outcomes focussed on the attendees departing with a feeling of unity as one cohesive fighting force ready to deliver hell upon their foe.

The Axis was still ascendant along the north African shoreline and in August 1942 a dispersal plan was initiated, lest the Allied army fail to keep the base at Alexandria secure. Whilst the 15th MTB Flotilla remained in place as an afterguard (with orders to torpedo and sink the immobilised French ships in Alexandria should there be a risk of them falling into German hands), the 7th MTB Flotilla was detached to Famagusta in Cyprus, where there were repair facilities which could be put to good use by Hennessy and his team. Once there, all the boats were given a rapid overhaul, and soon returned to Alexandria to be ready to support Field Marshal Montgomery's army, by now engaged in repelling German

Generalleutnant Rommel's Deutsches Afrika Korps as they pressed towards Cairo.

Further problems with MTB 62's steering gear required the engineering teams in Alexandria to conduct another round of repairs, which meant that the 10th and 15th MTB flotillas had to pick up extra tasking. Almost nightly, the crew of MTB 62 had to watch the departure at sunset of their fellow MTBs as they headed out to patrol the coast to prevent German and Italian resupply, or to drop British raiding parties behind Rommel's lines in order to disrupt him on shore.

In early September a plan was hatched to conduct a larger raid on Tobruk in Libya. Codenamed Operation *Agreement*, it involved four separate force groupings. Force C was to consist of 16 Motor Torpedo Boats, each carrying ten soldiers, accompanied by three Motor Launches (MLs) carrying army demolition parties. Force B was an army unit of troops specialising in long-range operations behind enemy lines; Force D was a supporting force of the cruiser HMS *Coventry* and four Destroyers. But of significance was the inclusion in Force A of Guy's former ship HMS *Sikh*, tasked along with her sister ship HMS *Zulu* with landing 350 Royal Marines each as the main thrust of the raid.

The plan for Operation *Agreement* was met with consternation by the Senior Officers of the 10th and 15th MTB flotillas. Raiding was not within the normal operational remit of torpedo boats, and there was no time to work up in the required tactics. In consequence, a regular RN Commander was appointed as Senior Officer MTBs for the operation. A few days later, on 12 September, Guy witnessed from the broken MTB 62 the departure of his fellow MTBs on a mission that was to prove problematic for the participants and generate lifelong memories.

The passage from Alexandria to the MTB objective at Mersa es Sciausc, just to the east of Tobruk, was conducted at a slow cruising speed of seven knots with the seven MTBs of the 10th Flotilla and the nine MTBs of the 15th Flotilla each in line-ahead, all boats following in the wake of their flotilla leader. Still undetected by the German and Italian navies, soon after dark on 13 September orders were given for each line of MTBs to turn landward to close their shoreline objective. There were no formal tactics for such an approach, so when the next order was received for the MTBs to increase speed to 24 knots the two RNVR MTB flotilla commanders decided to use the normal MTB tactic of incrementally adjusting their formations' speeds in five-knot steps; this allowed each boat to adjust her throttle to keep tightly in station on the boat ahead, while not stressing the engines, which had been near to idle for almost a day. However, the 'regular', temporary, RN Senior Officer MTBs saw this as insufficiently aggressive and overrode his two flotilla commanders by ordering a single step increase from seven to 24 knots. Within minutes the two formations began to break apart. With their complete lack of training in such a manoeuvre greatly accentuated by the pitch darkness in which they were trying to keep station, there was soon a disaggregated flotilla of four distinct MTB groups all heading roughly westward, instead of the single cohesive assault force demanded by the plan.

Guided in part by the flashes of guns over Tobruk, and hindered by under-powered visual signals that were being sent from shore by the soldiers of Force B, only two of the MTBs entered the cove at Mersa es Sciausc. MTB 314 ran aground and her crew plus soldiers were evacuated by MTB 261. Despite valiant efforts by the other MTB crews, the Axis defence proved too strong and the raid was curtailed.

By this time HMS *Sikh* was coming under very heavy fire as she attempted to land her Royal Marines to the north and west of Tobruk, so some MTBs were despatched to assist her. Operation *Agreement* was by this time becoming untenable, and the MTBs sent to aid *Sikh* proved no match for the Italian shore batteries pounding her with six-inch guns. As she tried to re-embark her troops, *Sikh* was disabled by enemy fire. HMS *Zulu* closed her to try to pull her away from the devastating shelling, but *Sikh* was mortally damaged. In the early hours of 14 September 1942, with her sister ship and Guy's fellow MTBs desperately trying to assist her, HMS *Sikh* succumbed to enemy fire and sank with the loss of 115 of Guy's former shipmates.

Back in Alexandria, Guy had to sit through the tales of this awful raid, hearing of the desperate and brave actions of his compatriots as he had been made, by mechanical unreliability of his boat, to sit out the party. Ships are like mistresses; you love them and you never forget them. Every ship has its own personality and generates memories which mean that service in any warship creates a lifelong bond with her (ships are called 'her' for a reason). Guy had been unable to help his former ship and had been unable to help his former shipmates, many of whom were now dead. What if he had been there?

Three weeks later, Guy was transferred to MTB 65, another Vosper 70-foot MTB. On 5 October 1942 he reported to Acting Lieutenant D Owen-Pawson, who had brought MTB 65 out of build. After failing her initial UK sea trials due to a gearbox defect, which had been repaired on the slip at Milford Haven, MTB 65 had been shipped from Cardiff on 21 June 1942 on board the SS *Telesfora de Larrinaga*. She was formally commissioned on 4 September 1942 just after her arrival in the Mediterranean. However, she was another sickly ship and was rarely available for operational patrols.

The 7th MTB Flotilla was on 25 January 1943 transferred to a new MTB base at HMS *Gregale* in Malta, the war in North Africa having now turned in favour of the Allies. This did nothing to unpick Guy's frustration at serving in a class of MTBs which, despite Guy's very best efforts, were still proving too unreliable to commit to serious operations. Indeed, during the winter of 1942 a decision was taken by Captain Coastal Forces Mediterranean to pay off Guy's MTB to allow extensive hull repairs; these lasted until autumn 1943, when on 27 September MTB 65 was finally recommissioned into the operational fleet.

But Guy had long since departed. Whilst Guy had been trying to nurse MTB 65 to a state of operational readiness, on the night of 15/16 February 1943 fellow MTB 77 had been involved in a desperate action operating with aircraft south of Marettimo Island near Sicily. Along with MTB 82, and three others, MTB 77 had attacked a strongly escorted enemy convoy, scoring a hit on one merchantman, with another 5,000-ton merchantman sunk by torpedoes from a cooperating Wellington bomber. After firing her torpedoes, Lieutenant John Brian Sturgeon (known as Brian), commanding MTB 77 with his Senior Officer (Lieutenant Hennessy) embarked, had turned towards another merchant ship to attack using depth charges. As they closed on their target, his First Lieutenant – Sub-Lieutenant D W Napier – was hit by enemy fire and killed in action while trying to release the port depth charge. On the morning of 16 February MTB 77 returned to Malta to discharge her dead, and she needed a new Second-in-Command.

Guy was given a 'discharge report' from his time in 70-foot MTBs, which stated that he was 'A very conscientious and capable officer who has done very well as 1st Lieutenant in MTBs 62 and 65. He is strongly recommended for Command.' It was signed by Lieutenant R Hennessy, who had by this time been working with Guy for over a year. As the flotilla leader, Hennessey did not command a boat of his own, but travelled for operations in a boat of his own choice. In practice this was most commonly MTB 77, so his decision to assign Guy to fight alongside him was testament to Guy's emerging reputation as a good officer.

MTB 77 was subtly different from Guy's former MTBs. She was a Vosper '72-foot 6-inch' MTB, just under a yard longer than his former boats, but powered by three of the much larger Packard V12 petrol engines. These produced a total of 4,050 brake horsepower, which gave MTB 77 a top speed of 39 knots. Part of a batch of 26 new MTBs ordered in May 1940, she was also fitted with larger fuel tanks and two additional 0.303-inch guns, one on each side of the bridge. To man these, she had three additional ship's company as standard. She was also much more reliable, and had already established for herself a fearsome reputation for success in combat.

With Guy assuming his new role on 17 February 1943, MTB 77 needed to be repaired prior to further action. Along with his Commanding Officer, Guy oversaw this maintenance, including the finishing touches, which on

Guy Hudson (fourth from left) with his new team. 'This one, my friends, may show me true to type, namely under the influence – but think it a little unkind!!!'
SB private collection

21 March 1943 required obeying the order for a new paint scheme. The Commander-in-Chief of the Royal Navy in the Mediterranean was becoming increasingly concerned about fratricide and directed that 'All MTBs, MGBs and MLs and HDMLS are to be painted yellow from the stem for six feet aft to facilitate recognition by our aircraft . . . All painting is to be complete by 1st April.'

As a respite from maintenance, as well as operations, the social life of coastal forces in Malta was as boisterous as their reputation in both HMS *Hornet* and HMS *Mosquito* demanded. Gin and tonic was still the fuel of choice, and the 'parties' were not just at sea. Guy was already an especially heavy drinker, annotating a picture of himself with his new crew, 'This one, my friends, may show me true to type, namely under the influence – but think it a little unkind!!!'

With MTB 77 close to readiness for operations, on 27 March 1943, ashore in HMS *Gregale*, Guy was unfortunate to trip over a carpet, putting his hand out to break his fall and striking a window pane ahead of him. It shattered, with a shard sinking deeply into his hand. This was treated by local medical staff such that he could remain at his post and continue to serve as First Lieutenant of the now repaired MTB 77. But the wound hurt.

On 29 March 1943, sporting her new colours, MTB 77 departed Malta to resume operations. Along with MTBs 95 (in which Hennessey had embarked), 61 and 84, she sailed to carry out operations off Sfax in Tunisia, with orders on completion to proceed to Tripoli. However, this was not to be Guy's night; poor Mediterranean weather got the better of them and on 30 March 1943 they returned to Malta.

His Majesty's Motor Torpedo Boat 77
SB private collection

During April, MTBs of the Mediterranean Coastal Forces carried out sweeps almost nightly, with largely inconclusive results, but brief contact was made on one occasion with enemy E-Boats. These sweeps constituted a continual menace to enemy communications and started to wear down their foe.

With the war in North Africa going very well for the Allied forces, a decision was made to strike forward, and on 20 April Captain Coastal Forces Mediterranean moved his operational headquarters from Malta to Algiers. To generate additional patrol time along the North African coast MTBs were forward deployed from Malta, with some based in Algiers and another base established in Sousse on the Tunisian coast.

On 25 April 1943, MTB 77 – now with an additional stripe on her bow restored to denote that the flotilla Senior Officer was embarked – sailed from Malta to embark on what was to be an especially intense period of operations working with US Patrol Torpedo boats and newly arrived Fairmile D-class MTBs (all with three-digit pennant numbers starting with a 6). Her home for the next month was to be Sousse, with its 18 MTB berths and very haphazard support facilities. She sailed with MTBs 61 and 76 initially in company, but 76 was forced to return to Malta with a defect. On arrival, however, MTB 77 was met by her new playmates – MTBs 635 and 639, newly arrived from Bone, augmenting MTBs 633 and 637, who were already alongside.

Having refuelled from the primitive facilities ashore, MTB 77 was ready for action. A night of rest was declared prior to her next patrol, but this was interrupted by an air raid in the early hours during which bombs were dropped in the sea and one or two behind the town. One enemy aircraft was shot down by night fighters and a second crashed into the sea eight to ten miles off the harbour entrance. The fighting had started.

The next morning the work of the Coastal Forces received a welcome boost. Commander-in-Chief Mediterranean made the following signal to all Coastal Forces craft: 'I am following the excellent work of the Coastal Forces with intense interest. Please assure them that they are contributing greatly to the difficulties of the enemy and the advance of our armies in Tunisia. Keep going full out.'

That evening, on 27 April 1943, MTB 77 departed at 1730 'full out' with two others so as to be in position to operate from first light off the Tunisian coast north of Ras Mahmur. They were warned that the operation was in the nature of an experiment and that undue risks were not to be run, and they were ordered to return to Sousse if air opposition was too heavy.

The patrol was certainly eventful. MTB 639 was engaged by shore batteries, caught fire and sank with the loss of the 32nd MTB Flotilla's Senior Officer (Lieutenant Stewart Gould DSC and Bar RNVR) and three ratings. MTB 633 had lost two engines as a result of the same enemy action and limped back to Sousse, having recovered the bodies of her fallen comrades. But MTB 77 had survived and was ready to fight again.

The next day the gallant Gould was buried at Sousse. Departing at 1730 that evening, along with MTBs 264, 61 and 75, MTB 77 swept the coast as far as Sidi Daoud, this time meeting no enemy resistance and returning to Sousse on 30 April before the weather closed in and made further operations untenable. This became part of a pattern of life for the MTB force based there. Under the inspirational leadership of Commander C Thomas Royal Navy, facilities in the Souse temporary naval base were improving with every day, as demolition and reconstruction began to enhance the number of available berths. But the weather was becoming the driving factor for operational employment of the coastal MTB force.

After a weather-imposed night in harbour on 1 May 1943, the following evening saw the seas calm down enough for another patrol. Just before sunset on 2 May MTBs 77 (with Hennessey embarked as Senior Officer), 61, 75 and 264 departed for another relatively uneventful sweep along the coast, although they were illuminated by enemy starshell between 2130 and 2145. A rest night was then ordered for 3 May, with another patrol commenced on 4 May and scheduled for Sidi Daoud. However, weather once again got the better of these small craft and MTBs 77, 264 and 61 returned to harbour shortly afterwards.

The MTB patrol for the night of 5 May uneventfully headed towards Cape Bon, with Guy's MTB 77 again in the lead along with MTBs 61 and 264. They returned to be greeted by reinforcements arriving from Malta with MTBs 95 and 62 (Guy's first operational boat) now alongside in Sousse. Throwing MTB 62 straight into the operational schedule, MTB 77 that evening led MTBs 82 and 62 on a three-boat patrol along the coast towards Cape Bon, to be blooded by inaccurate enemy aircraft bombing at 2125 as they passed 3.5 miles due east of Kelibia.

Life in Sousse had started to become a routine, with two nights of operations followed by a night of rest, regulated by the drill of the MTBs nominated for the next patrol being briefed by HQ on the next set of requirements, developing and briefing their detailed plans, then sailing just as darkness fell to do their bit to win the war. Every night teams of 30 to 50 young sailors, spread across three or four nearly identical boats, would steam towards enemy waters, drawing moral strength from their mutual trust and interdependence.

Both Germans and Italians were still active in the area, and on 7 May enemy mines were located in the vicinity of Sousse. MTB officers were extremely familiar with the threat from mines, as their training included fast minelaying operations. So it was with increased trepidation that on the evening of 8 May Lieutenant Hennessey embarked in Guy's MTB 77 to lead his force out on their next patrol. All units were under strict orders to keep to swept minefield channels, with standard mine countermeasures demanding that they head as far offshore as practicable and then remain in deep (less mineable) water. But the orders for MTBs 77 and 61, together with the United States' PT 203,[7] were to patrol 'close inshore' between Cape Bon and Kelibia. The operational situation ashore was becoming

---

[7] Dudley Pope in *Flag 4* (London: Kimber, 1954) lists this as PT 209. However, the official war diary by Commander-in-Chief Mediterranean clearly states in multiple entries that it was PT 203, as does Robert J Bulkley in his account of US PT boat operations At *Close Quarters* (Washington: Naval History Division, 1962). I have used the ship data from the official Royal Navy record as verified by the US account.

extremely tense, with the Axis desperate to achieve maritime resupply to their beleaguered forces, so these orders were augmented by a crystal-clear signal from Commander-in-Chief Mediterranean to all his Destroyers and other patrolling forces: 'Sink, burn and destroy. Let nothing pass.' They sailed with zero doubt in their minds as to their conduct. However, with the MTBs employing the standard tactics of steaming to their area, then running on their silent centreline engine until an enemy was located, the order to 'crash-start wing engines' was on that night not forthcoming.

Under the new codename of Operation *Retribution*, they had so far met no enemy forces, but the patrol the following evening, consisting of the same team, pushed itself a little too hard. Trundling on her silent engine close

Guy Hudson SB private collection

inshore past the enemy-held Fort Kelibia, MTB 61 peeked into the harbour to see if an attack on some reported enemy barges was worthwhile. Unfortunately she ran herself aground.

'Close inshore' meant they were only 200 yards from enemy territory when they became fast on the seabed, and they had unfortunately chosen to do so right under the gaze of Axis soldiers in the fort. The enemy initially failed to appreciate that the now stationary boats below them were British and American, believing them to be their own forces attempting to re-enter the port under cover of darkness. So the initial efforts by MTB 77 and PT 203 to rescue their comrades were conducted without interference.

The role of First Lieutenant then saw Guy assume another sailor's hat of managing the upper-deck seamanship teams as they tried to tow MTB 61 off the shoreline. But she was stuck fast. His compatriot over in MTB 61, Sub-Lieutenant F Johnson, was leading the standard actions in such a situation, including mustering the crew to stand on the stern in an attempt to lift the bow off the seabed, followed by ditching ammunition (including unprimed depth charges) in an attempt to lighten their load. Their last possible action should have been to start their wing engines, but they would have to do so in the full knowledge that the distinct roaring noise of these British powerhouses would be recognised instantly by the enemy soldiers above.

As the smaller of the two boats still afloat, PT 203 then closed MTB 61 and relayed an order from Hennessey that MTB 61 should be abandoned and destroyed. Johnson duly took the bag of confidential books and sunk it in the deepest water he could find around the grounded wreck, whilst the Commanding Officer, Lieutenant T J Bligh RNVR, commenced the scuttling process. With the engine rooms evacuated, Petty Officer Motor Mechanic Matthews filled the engine room bilges with petrol and Bligh stood by with a 'Very Pistol' flare gun, ready to deflagrate his ship.

With PT 203 about 200 yards away, as close as she could get, the crew of MTB 61 commenced abandoning ship. By now the enemy were inquisitive and were firing an occasional burst of investigatory fire towards the stranded craft. Just as the last of the crew were entering the water the enemy fire became more intense, although the Germans could not depress their big guns sufficiently to bring larger calibre shells to bear. Bligh fired his flare into the engine room, which not only distracted the enemy but also blew the stern clean off the beleaguered MTB . . . with Bligh still standing on it! He was thrown into the water and started to swim away from the abandoned conflagration, which was now under heavy and sustained enemy bombardment.

PT 203's second officer, Ensign Ernest W Olson US Naval Reserve, jumped into the water to help the British crew and picked up all but one of MTB 61's team. Leading Stoker F Adshead had been seen in the water halfway between his boat and PT 203, but now could not be located. He was never found. The others were distributed between PT 203 and MTB 77; they headed back to Sousse to debrief their night's adventures and pray for another close colleague who they convinced themselves had been captured as a prisoner of war, but who deep down they knew had drowned only yards from rescue.

Operation *Retribution* demanded unprecedented effort, so the thought of a night to recover never entered the minds of the MTB crews in Sousse. After welcoming MTBs 76, 78 and 309 as new reinforcements from Malta, at 1730 on the evening of 9 May Guy's boat, again with Hennessey embarked to command his flotilla, departed with MTBs 75 and 82 for patrol between Kelibia and Cape Bon. By 2115 they had established themselves in a silent patrol pattern close off the coast, watching the battle ashore as the air over the town was pinpricked by flares and anti-aircraft tracer fired at passing aeroplanes.

Just after 0300 it was MTB 77's turn to creep into Kelibia harbour, where she saw one of the 80-foot barges sought by MTB 61 the previous night. Guy's Commanding Officer, Lieutenant Brian Sturgeon, played it perfectly. In an ideal firing position right under the noses of enemy sentries in the fort above, at 0315 MTB 77 unleashed her deadly payload of two torpedoes, each set to their shallowest running depths of two and three feet respectively. With weapons in the water, 77's gunners unleashed hell on the enemy, supported by the 0.5-inch gunners in MTBs 75 and 82. One torpedo struck home, the target barge sinking under the deluge of water sent skyward by the torpedo's exploding warhead, quickly followed by a further two large explosions credited to the very accurate shooting of the gunnery ratings.

Concurrently, the other patrol for the night of 9 May had equal success, attacking some small craft off Cape Bon and taking 36 enemy prisoners. And by sunrise all six patrolling MTBs returned safely to Sousse to celebrate their tactical victory.

By daylight the crews of the small boats celebrated, debriefed, refuelled, topped up on ammunition, repaired their battle damage and got some rest, before once more briefing for departure just before sunset. With Guy's MTB 77 again in the van, accompanied by MTBs 75 and 82 as her wingmen, they resumed their attacking efforts in the now rich hunting grounds between Cape Bon and Kelibia. They were under specific orders to stay as close inshore as possible, the patrol areas for British Destroyers having been moved towards the Tunisian coast as part of the Allied strategy to strangle enemy forces still holding out.

As they glided along the coast the light from flares ashore pinpointed a number of small boats lying in Kelibia roads, which Hennessey declared as their targets for the night. In a classic MTB action, they formed up for torpedo attack and a pair of torpedoes was unleashed by the flotilla, one of which was seen to explode. All three boats then closed for follow-up gunfire attacks on the enemy craft, which were unable to muster any return shots.

The MTBs returned to Sousse victorious, with another superb patrol under their belts. After months of frustration, the Coastal Forces campaign at sea was now in full flow and contributing to the success of the Allied operation, although there was disappointment that the enemy was not attempting a mass evacuation by sea that could provide an even more target-rich environment. However, in his war diary summarising this phase of the campaign, Commander-in-Chief Mediterranean opined that 'it is hoped that the nightly presence of MTBs close off the coast may have helped to influence' the decision not to evacuate by sea.[8]

Potentially prematurely, but also as a considerable boost to morale, the returning boats were greeted with a copy of a signal received by the Allied Commander-in-Chief from His Majesty the King:

> Throughout the six months during which you have been in Command of the Allied Forces in North Africa, I have watched with admiration the progress of operations on Sea, on Land and in the air. Under your leadership, forces diverse in Nationality and race have been knit into one united and successful whole. Their task has not been easy and the resistance of the enemy has been determined and desperate. But now, with the capture of Tunis and Bizerta, your campaign is almost concluded; the last enemy forces in Africa are being captured or destroyed and the debt of Dunkirk repaid. On behalf of all my peoples, I express to you, as Supreme Commander of Allied Forces, and to all ranks under your Command our Heartfelt congratulations on your Victory.

But such congratulations could not be allowed to distract them from their operational duties, and at 1530 on 11 May 1943 Guy's MTB 77 again led MTBs 75 and 82 out through the swept channel off Sousse and towards the enemy hold-outs at Kelibia. By 1801 they had achieved their first success, sinking a small white boat. They closed the wreckage and at 1835 recovered five prisoners from its life raft.

With prisoners under guard below, at 1927 they closed the coast near Kharba and flashed Morse code to communicate with some tanks ashore. The tanks had been correctly identified as friendly and they updated Hennessey and his team on the situation ashore; the whole peninsula was now in Allied hands.

---

[8]   Commander-in-Chief Mediterranean War Diary, May–September 1943, entry summarising May 1943.

Resuming their patrol, it was eerily quiet. Kelibia roads still contained a few watercraft, but all were damaged or abandoned. At 2115 they captured a further prisoner, an Italian, before departing to patrol along the coast. After spending a few hours off Ras Idda in the silent MTB running posture, they headed south-east back to Kelibia to again investigate events ashore. There were no signs of life in the town, but strangely there was also no sign of MTB 61, abandoned and burnt out a few days earlier.

The MTBs resumed boarding of vessels in the anchorage, collecting some items of equipment they thought could be of intelligence value, before arriving back at Sousse just before 1000. Fellow MTBs 78, 76 and 75 also returned from patrol off Kelibia, where 13 German prisoners had been captured from a fishing boat 12 miles east of Rasel Mihir. The forward base at Sousse now had another 19 enemy mouths to feed.

Achieving victory in war requires guile, courage, ruthlessness, but also very sound administration. The achievements of the MTBs in conducting sustained operations from a poorly equipped forward base was widely recognised, with Commander-in-Chief Mediterranean singling out Guy's unit for specific praise when he noted that 'considering the lack of facilities, the [MTBs] ran with considerable reliability especially MTBs 77, 75 and 61.' But they were in fact being held together by the best efforts of dedicated and resourceful engineers instead of by sound engineering practice, so on 12 May orders were received for the 7th MTB Flotilla to return to Malta, where it would be repaired before joining the 32nd MTB Flotilla and the 20th MGB Flotilla.

The following day, on 13 May 1943, German General von Arnim surrendered his forces to the Allies and Operation *Retribution* came to a successful end. A hundred and fifty thousand German and Italian troops were taken prisoner along with captured tanks, artillery, ammunition and transport vehicles. The MTBs at Sousse duly packed up their belongings to return to their main base in Malta. With Hennessey embarked in his favourite MTB 77, Guy and his team sailed from Sousse on the evening of 14 May, arriving at HMS *Gregale* the following morning. In the period

April to May 1943 Guy's MTB was officially the busiest of the 7th Flotilla, conducting ten directed operations off enemy territory. The boat and crew needed some maintenance.

As part of the reorganisation of Mediterranean MTBs, Lieutenant Hennessey was promoted to Lieutenant Commander and appointed CO of HMS *Gregale*. He was relieved as Senior Officer 7th MTB Flotilla by Lieutenant A C B Blomfield DSC Royal Navy. He set about optimising the operational efficiency across all his units and, on 24 May 1943, Guy was reassigned by Hennessey to work alongside him in HMS *Gregale* as 'spare Commanding Officer', instantly ready to step aboard any Motor Torpedo or Motor Gun Boat from any of the three Malta flotillas should they be in need of a relief captain; was this to be his time to command? But his injured hand was becoming an increasing handicap and it needed treatment that was unavailable in the austere conditions of besieged Malta.

Reinforced by the sustained successes of the Mediterranean, as well as those of the MTBs and MGBs in the UK, the reputation of the Coastal Forces was becoming legendary. On 30 May 1943 Winston Churchill saw fit to recognise this by sending a message to all officers and men in the Coastal Forces:

I have noted with admiration the work of the light coastal forces in the North Sea, in the Channel and more recently in the Mediterranean.

Both in offence and defence the fighting zeal and the professional skill of officers and men have maintained the great tradition built up by many generations of British seamen.

As our strategy becomes more strongly offensive, the task allotted to the coastal forces will increase in importance, and the area of operations will widen.

I wish to express my heartfelt congratulations to you and all on what you have done in the past, and complete confidence that you will sustain the same high standards until complete victory has been gained over all our enemies.

Winston S Churchill

In the Royal Navy, the toast after supper every Thursday is to 'a bloody war and a sickly season'. This is based on the fact that both events are good for promotion. A bloody war allows younger officers to display their valour whilst their seniors are killed in action, freeing up promotion slots; a sickly season sees the older and more senior members of the wardroom die of disease while the younger survive to take their place. The first few weeks of June failed to deliver the former to Guy, with a lack of enemy action for the Malta MTBs. However, he fell victim to the latter. Guy's call to command was not forthcoming, whilst his hand was getting steadily worse. On 17 June 1943 Guy was discharged from the 7th Flotilla, receiving two glowing reports from Hennessey:

> Termination of Appointment: A very capable officer with a sound knowledge of Service matters. Very hard working, he gets on with the job without having to be told. Bearing in Action good with more than average powers of endurance. Very popular in the Flotilla. Highly recommended for Command of a Coastal Forces Craft (MTB or MGB). Extremely loyal. Recommended for accelerated promotion.

And on a second sheet:

> Recommendation for Accelerated Promotion AFO 425/42: This officer is above average as a Sub Lieutenant RNVR having a far greater knowledge of service matters than most. He is very hard working and can always be relied upon to do any job he is given efficiently. The best First-Lieutenant of an MTB I have met in five years.

Both were supportively, yet perfunctorily, countersigned by Captain G Hubback Royal Navy, Captain Coastal Forces Mediterranean: 'Concur'.

His hand now in need of urgent medical attention, Guy evacuated from Malta, arriving back in Britain a few days later. He was sent straight to the nearest proper hospital.

Precision Tactics

—◦◦—

Guy was admitted to the Royal Naval Hospital Plymouth on 30 June 1943, where he was diagnosed with neurotmesis of the left ulnar nerve. He needed to allow nature to heal the wound without the distractions of firing torpedoes at Germans, or of recovering enemy prisoners from life rafts, and the next day he was discharged and granted 21 days' sick leave. He had been away for over a year and had much catching up to do, so he seized the opportunity to visit his family.

The medical staff monitored his treatment and he was on 28 July 1943 transferred to the Royal Navy's rehabilitation centre at Sherborne in Dorset. After a month of highly effective physiotherapy he was on 25 August 1943 granted another 14 days' sick leave prior to a medical board of survey scheduled for 8 September.

Rather problematically for an MTB officer, especially one with the operational experience Guy had gained during the North Africa campaign, he was not considered fit for sea and the board of survey assigned him for three months' 'shore service'. This allowed him to recuperate sufficiently such that on 8 December 1943 he was resurveyed and found fit for sea service, but 'not in small craft for nine months'.

During this period he received the great news that he had been promoted. He was listed in the *London Gazette* on 10 September 1943 as 'Promoted to Temporary Lieutenant, with a seniority of 1 September 1943'. He then joined his next unit, at HMS *Bee* in Weymouth, as a navigation instructor specialising in coastal forces tactics.

HMS *Bee* had been commissioned on 1 September 1942 under Admiralty Fleet Order 4469/42. It was designated as a working-up base for Coastal

*Lieutenant Guy Hudson, wearing 'Coastal Forces rig',
with his mother, Doris 'Polly' Hudson*
SB private collection

Forces and occupied a hotel, the Pavilion theatre and a row of boarding houses along the seafront in Weymouth. From their shorebase, training officers supervised the working up and then final certifications of MTBs and MGBs immediately before they joined their front-line flotillas.

Guy took over from Lieutenant P N Hood RNVR, who had set up the navigation section of the school and who had pioneered some of the exacting navigation techniques required when maintaining accurate locational records of fast-manoeuvring Motor Torpedo and Motor Gun Boats. Guy had a hard act to follow, but he was to rise to this challenge by applying his sharp intellect combined with a superb attention to detail.

But the memory of his first day in his new role was to be tinged with sadness. As has already been explained, sailors form very close attachments to their ships, and they remain attached to former ships throughout their careers. Reading of the successes of a former unit always inspires a hint of pride, with memories returning of your part in generating the unit's reputation and fighting spirit. In equal measure, learning of the demise of a former ship instantly brings back memories of what she had done for you, when she had kept you safe, and how she had helped you through some random scrape or two. The coastal forces report for 8 September would thus have made sad reading for Guy. MTB 77, from which he had torpedoed the enemy, silently glided past the guns of Axis fortresses and rescued his close colleagues from the clutches of capture, had that night been conducting a very special mission off Vibo Valentia, Calabria, delivering Flag Officer Sicily (Rear Admiral R R McGrigor) to visit the Allied landings. A German bomb had exploded two feet from her starboard quarter and ripped open her underwater hull, causing her to sink. Fortunately all her crew were rescued by ML1128, but, having survived 33 operations, MTB 77 had finally succumbed to the Germans.

Only a month after Guy joined, on 16 October 1943, HMS *Bee* was moved to Holyhead, further from the occasional but encumbering interference of German E-Boat patrols in the English Channel and also to distance itself from the preparations for D-Day, which were to become a dominant feature of Guy's service. The former base supply ship in Holyhead, HMS *Torch*, was paid off to allow *Bee* to be stood up correctly, with a concurrent merger of the roles of Naval-Officer-in-Charge Holyhead and Commanding Officer HMS *Bee*.

It was during this period that, in addition to his duties as a navigation instructor, Guy met with Lieutenant Phillip Gordon Lee RNVR, at this stage a twice-decorated Motor Gun Boat officer who had established for himself a reputation as an exceptional MGB commander. In August 1942 he had been awarded a Distinguished Service Cross for his part in an action against German R-Boats off Dover, earning a bar to his DSC in May 1943 for an MGB action against German trawlers and more R-Boats.

Phillip Lee had been assigned to HMS *Bee* three weeks after Guy, and before long they were collaborating, developing highly innovative tactics to use radars fitted to Frigates in order to control Motor Torpedo and Motor Gun Boats into close action with the enemy.

A fellow MTB officer, Lieutenant Richard Guy Fison RNVR, had in July 1943 established at Kingswear, near Dartmouth, a shore radar control station from which teams of radar plotters and Direction Officers provided information to patrolling MTBs regarding potential enemy craft. A recent advance in radar had changed the former technique of determining contact range from a linear display, and contact bearing information from a separate readout of the aerial's direction; the Plan Position Indicator, or PPI display, was now a single circular display with the radar aerial in the middle, bearing information read from a calibrated scale around the edge, and range information directly proportional to the distance of the displayed contact from the centre of the circular display. This was revolutionary. Using simple plotting techniques it was now possible to provide very rapid information to subordinate MTBs at sea on their position relative to any possible enemy, along with very precise information on the course that the MTBs should steer in order to intercept their quarry.

Phillip Lee and Guy Hudson wanted to translate this battle-winning tactic from use only around the coast, where the radar aerial was geographically fixed on shore, to a mobile platform such as a Frigate.

To do so they refined what was called the Action Information Organisation, or AIO. This was a highly streamlined system of gathering tactical information, but in the case of Guy and Phillip Lee's design it was within an onboard plotting room and derived from a variety of sensors, radios and other sources such as intelligence, operational orders and plans. By fusing this information in a strictly coordinated manner, they could provide the Senior Officer, known as the Surface Force Direction Officer (or SFDO), with enough data to allow highly informed judgements to be made regarding disposition and control of assigned subordinate forces which could lead to rapid and successful engagements with the enemy. The key revolutionary factor in this work was that it all happened in a plotting room that generally had no windows, which were unnecessary if their AIO was functioning correctly. This was a radical departure from hundreds of years of naval practice whereby ships were fought from their bridge, by the captain as the Senior Officer, with all information being passed to him as he looked for himself at the physical enemy and at the tactical situation.

By the spring of 1944, anticipating Operation *Neptune* (the naval element of D-Day), the widely understood fighter grid system had been made universal in the channel in order to ease directing of coastal forces patrols and to prevent fratricide. Further measures to reduce the risk of misidentification included fitting the new Indicator Friend or Foe (IFF) radar system (type 253) to all MTBs, with radio interrogators (type 242) fitted to Frigates, but results were disappointing and more traditional methods of very careful plotting and tracking were still to be used. Further work was urgently needed in order to refine the tactics of mutual cooperation required for the liberation of mainland Europe. Guy and Phillip Lee set about this task with dedication and a single-minded resolve to succeed.

Whilst all this tactical development was going on, Guy continued to maintain his intimate understanding of MTB activities on the front line. He was an MTB officer through and through, part of the incredibly tight-knit community of the Coastal Forces team, with many officers generating enviable reputations. It was thus with great sadness that Guy learnt that his inspirational former Commanding Officer, Lieutenant J Brian Sturgeon DSC RNVR, had been killed in action on the night of 2/3 April 1944. Brian Sturgeon had driven MTB 77 with exceptional zeal, earning a Distinguished Service Cross in June 1943 (just after Guy's departure) for gallantry leading to the surrender of the islands of Pantelleria and Lampedusa. He had later been appointed as Senior Officer of the 24th MTB Flotilla, taking up his new command at the end of March 1944. However, on his very first patrol as flotilla Senior Officer he succumbed to the enemy when leading a two-boat patrol consisting of MTB 242 (in which he was embarked) and MTB 81. The patrol encountered an I-Boat (a 20-ton landing craft) and attacked it vigorously; the I-Boat returned fire and Brian was killed instantly by a single bullet. Brian Sturgeon DSC was the next day buried with full naval honours on the Croatian island of Vis, later being moved to the Commonwealth war cemetery at Belgrade. Guy had lost another friend with whom he had created many memories and survived many close scrapes.

A month after this sad news, Guy and Phillip Lee were transferred from HMS *Bee* to the Coastal Forces base at HMS *Hornet* at Gosport, opposite the huge naval base at Portsmouth and adjacent to the headquarters of Captain Coastal Forces Channel. Guy's report from his time at HMS *Bee* reflected his persona, and also his dual task of training the next generation of MTB officers in the techniques of accurate navigation whilst concurrently developing surface force direction plotting techniques:

> A most hardworking and thorough young Officer. Full of ideas, plenty of initiative, he has at all times done his best, and a good best, for the improvement of pilotage, plotting and navigation in Coastal Forces.

> Has great charm of manner but is by nature slightly retiring. Nevertheless I have every confidence that he would do well in Command.

Guy had also made many new and enduring friends. Each new MTB or MGB crew spent between four and eight weeks working up at HMS *Bee*, and Guy would have seen dozens of crews arrive fresh-faced, then depart a few weeks later ready for war. Preparing a ship for war was a team effort by the ship's company and the shore-based training staff, who delivered the essential classroom lessons as well as going to sea to guide successful tactical execution. And, with shared accommodation and dining facilities ashore, the camaraderie throughout the coastal forces was exceptionally strong. Moving from training back to the front line, Guy was again going to be working with many very close friends who were to rely on his tactics to keep them alive.

Planning and training for D-Day was going on all along the south coast. On 3 May 1944, whilst Guy was on a week's leave between appointments, Exercise *Fabius* took place off Selsey Bill, which was assaulted by 'Forces

G, J and S'. In a rehearsal for D-Day, they were screened by an outer 'forward' layer of MTBs and inner 'rear' layer of Destroyers, Frigates, sloops and Corvettes, and there was a free bombing area off the French coast. The Germans paid no attention to the exercise, but at 0715 MTBs 708 and 720 were shot up by British Beaufighters returning from patrol; MTB 708 was sunk and MTB 720 was badly damaged. There were 16 casualties. The need for effective coordination between surface forces and their air counterparts could not have been more starkly illustrated.

Despite these losses, the exercise was deemed a great success but led to the realisation that the high density of coastal forces screening against German interference could not be maintained for Operation *Neptune* itself, unless better tactics were employed.

Guy had not been available for Exercise *Fabius*, but he had been making the most of his time. He had fallen in love with Section Officer Sylvia Mary Price, of the Women's Auxiliary Air Force. In fact, Guy had known Sylvia for many years, having been introduced through his beloved grandfather Richard, who was both a professional acquaintance and a friend of Sylvia's father. With D-Day approaching, and the country facing an uncertain future, Guy proposed to Sylvia and she accepted, just in time for Guy to depart for his next assignment.

On 10 May 1944, Guy formally joined his new unit. His service record noted the nature of his new mission: 'Special Service with Captain Coastal Forces Channel as a "Surface Force Direction Officer"'. He and Phillip Lee needed to get their surface force direction tactics battle-ready, and quickly.

A decision had already been taken that Captain-class Frigates, acquired by the British under the UK–US Lend–Lease programme, would be the ideal ships for surface force direction. They had the required radar, and they also had a plotting room just behind the bridge in which the Surface Force Direction Officer could station himself with his team of 14 action data compilers. This space was critical to accommodate both the equipment and the practitioners of Guy and Lee's tactics, with final team composition honed through months of training, trials and evaluation whilst they were serving together on HMS *Bee*. To deliver success in combat, Guy's required surface force direction team consisted of:

Surface Force Direction Officer (Guy's role): responsible for the interception, tactical planning and passing of enemy information to attached units.[9]

Operations Room Officer (ORO): supplies the SFDO with all necessary information.

Local Operational Plot Officer (LOP Officer): in charge of the local operational plot and supplies the ORO with the necessary information for making enemy reports.

PPI Operator: identifies and reports all radar contact ranges and bearings.

Radar Plotter 2: plots radar contacts onto the LOP.

Radar Plotter 3: plots the general operations plot and assists on the local operations plot.

'Y' Operator: operates communications intercept equipment, informing the SFDO and command of all information received.

Narrative Recorder: maintains a complete record of all events, and assists the ORO in keeping the bridge informed.

Telegraphist 1: operates the primary radio telephone (R/T), passing signals as directed by the SFDO.

Telegraphist 2: monitors the R/T frequency of adjacent forces, ensuring total situational awareness of surrounding events.

Telegraphist 3: operates the master Morse-code wireless telegraphy (W/T) key (for reports to shore).

---

[9] The detailed job description given in the *Coastal Forces Periodic Review* for January to March 1945 goes on to stress the requirement for an SFDO to have thorough knowledge of assigned unit tactics. It also states that during E-Boat interceptions the SFDO may station himself at the PPI display and directly read bearing and range information in order to reduce the delay in their transmission by radio to directed forces.

Coder: codes and decodes all messages transmitted or received on W/T.

Petty Officer Telegraphist: assists the SFDO and ORO with passing of signals, managing all telegraphy staff.

QH or Loran Operator: fixes (i.e. plots the position of) the ship as required.

To maintain the highest possible levels of precision and focus on detecting the enemy, there was an additional team member:

Relief Operator: a fully qualified PPI operator to take over the duties on the PPI, changing every 30 minutes.

The drill Guy and Phillip Lee had developed relied on the seamless passage of information between all the members of the team above. Once the team were established, with plots of all known friendly forces in both their own and adjacent areas, they relied on the PPI operator to maintain their knowledge of the whereabouts of their own assigned units as well as identifying new, unknown, radar contacts. Any unexpected radar echo was to be plotted on the LOP and the SFDO was to be given all possible information to make a decision as to its hostility: was there any communications intercept information to indicate hostility; was the ship's position exactly accurate or could there be a navigation error; were all assigned units exactly where reported; had any adjacent units strayed into the wrong area? The SFDO had to make rapid decisions, and then commit assigned forces to intercept and destroy any enemies. The darkness in which almost all MTB operations were undertaken meant that the SFDO was the sole point of responsibility; the element of surprise was critical in delivering mission success, and a surprise lethal attack would often be over before visual identification could be achieved.

Achieving such a surprise attack required all the assigned units to remain poised in carefully planned silent loitering positions, known precisely to the SFDO. Once a decision to attack was made, the SFDO would issue his orders through the telegraphist. The chosen MTB formation would crash-start their wing engines, and they would steer the precise course calculated by the SFDO. They would proceed utterly blind through the pitch darkness, until at ranges of typically 500 to 1,000 yards they would be able to see hints of their target, taking over the intercept as soon as such visual contact was made. Occasionally their small radars could help, but with effective detection ranges of only one to two miles, this could not be relied upon. The SFDO's job was thus to get the subordinate MTBs into a firing position as efficiently as possible.

Additional roles of the SFDO included coordinating with assigned Destroyers for the firing of starshell or other illumination, always in such a manner that the attacking MTBs could not be seen; this was usually by ordering the firing of illuminants to a position which would be 'behind' the enemy, as seen by the Allied attackers. A failure of this part of any attack could expose the MTBs to a hail of unwanted enemy fire.

This was a high-stakes task, with margins for error measured in only a few degrees or a few yards. The role of SFDO was not for the faint-hearted.

For their tactics to work they needed control ships. The Admiralty initially assigned four Captain-class Frigates to this role, all of which were despatched to Portsmouth to be fitted with the required equipment. The Commanding Officer of HMS *Stayner*, Lieutenant Commander Harry John Hall RNR, was the Senior Officer of this four-ship flotilla, with HM Ships *Thornborough*, *Retalik* and *Trollope* making up the group. In mid-May 1944, in addition to the radar that was already installed, each was fitted with 20- and 40-millimetre guns, a coastal forces radio suite, and a precise navigation aid nicknamed 'Mickey Mouse'.

After the events of Exercise *Fabius* it was necessary to implement training for the new surface direction teams as well as the MTBs they would be controlling. Guy, together with Phillip Lee and Lieutenant M G Duff RNVR, devised two critical training events: Harbour Control Exercise *Naylor*, and Ship Control Exercise *Nonslip*. Both exercises were delivered to MTBs of the 13th, 14th, 35th, 53rd and 64th flotillas, all of whom would be under SDFO direction during Operation *Neptune*.

Exercises *Naylor* and *Nonslip* proved to be of such great success that the Admiralty, given the acute anxiety of poor radar coverage along the French coast, decided to allocate four more Frigates to augment the radar control ship force, but only once their cross-channel escort duties were completed after the initial phase of the assault. HM Ships *Duff*, *Torrington*, *Seymour* and *Riou* were given the additional equipment needed, accompanied by some very rapid training delivered by Guy and Phillip Lee. This training allowed two further control officers to be integrated into the force; Lieutenant H A J Hollings DSC RNVR was to work alongside Phillip Lee, and Lieutenant C J Wright RANVR was to become Guy's sidekick.

The culmination of this seismic effort was Exercise *Cantab*, a 'full-scale' rehearsal of Naval Commander Eastern Task Force's defence organisation from a supposed forward deployed base in France. With their assigned Captain-class Frigates still completing their modifications, HMS *Scylla* was assigned control of the 55th and 29th MTB flotillas, with additional British MTBs acting as enemy forces. Although some of the very well-handled simulated enemy did manage to penetrate the outer layer of HMS *Scylla's* defensive screen, these attackers were defeated and the entire surface control concept proven. It is of historical note that, as written in the exercise report, '[British] Coastal Forces representing E-Boats were carrying out their attacks when genuine teutonic E-Boats were being held some 20 miles to the Southward . . . it must be mentioned that the defending forces restrained themselves from opening fire on this occasion.'[10]

These training events transformed into operations when, on the night of 1 June, a control ship, together with two MTB units, was despatched to mid-channel as a live anti-E-Boat patrol. The mission was, for proving the procedures, a success, although no E-Boats were encountered.

---

[10] Report on Operation Overlord – Portsmouth Command, 765/0/5, 12 September 1944 – Enclosure III (Coastal Forces), para. 49

Shortly before D-Day, Guy and Phillip's team of control officers received two further augmentations. Lieutenant Christopher Dreyer Royal Navy was a regular officer, unusual in the Coastal Forces, who had served with Guy whilst in the Mediterranean. He was already a legend in the closed world of MTBs, having been in command of the 3rd MTB Flotilla in 1940, aged 21, when at the start of the evacuation of British troops from France he had received an order to 'nip over to Dunkirk and see what you can do'. On 1 June 1940, when rescuing survivors from the sinking Destroyer HMS *Keith* off the coast of France, he became one of the most junior Flag Captains to fly an Admiral's flag in action, when he recovered Rear Admiral Wake-Walker; his crew immediately improvised an Admiral's flag from a tea towel and some red paint, proudly flying it from the MTB's rigging.

The final member of their team joined on 3 July 1944; Lieutenant Richard Guy Fison RNVR was formally seconded from his radar control unit at Kingswear. Although Fison had been working on shore-based radar control of Motor Torpedo Boats in the south-west area, including the use by subordinate MTBs of their own radar to refine attacking solutions, his expertise could now be better used by Guy Hudson and Phillip Lee.

By 5 June 1944, the day before the commencement of Operation *Overlord* (of which Operation *Neptune* was the maritime effort), 74 out of the 76 Motor Torpedo Boats assigned to the Portsmouth Command were ready for operations: 97 percent of available forces. This was the culmination of a remarkable effort by engineers and crews to be ready for the fight. Despite the strong wind on the night of 5/6 June, they deployed in full strength for the first night of Operation *Overlord*, conducting escorts of the assault formation's spearhead, diversionary operations and a minelay. Two control ships coordinated MTB operations off Pointe de Barfleur, but no surface actions developed.

The following morning, and almost every morning thereafter for the first few weeks, the control ships would shepherd their flock of assigned MTBs back to Portsmouth, where MTBs were refuelled and rearmed, and control officers would muster at HMS *Hornet* or the adjacent HMS *Dolphin*, to debrief the events of the night before as well as re-brief ready for the next night. This preparation started to be of value from the second night of the assault, with first encounters between control ships, MTBs and E-Boats setting a new standard that was to repeat itself every night until the end of August. MTB engagements of the enemy become common, ferocious and deadly.

By 7 June 1944 the German E- and R-Boats were out in force. British and Canadian MTBs attacked, driving one German R-Boat into a minefield off Le Havre where it blew itself up. MTBs 624 and 682 scored a draw against these targets, 624 becoming holed in her petrol tank and 682 taking five wounded before the engagement terminated.

Overall the British MTBs were upholding the very best traditions of the Coastal Forces, engaging the enemy with verve and determination. The Germans were unable to penetrate the defensive wall created by Guy and Phillip Lee's tactics, but they were scoring some painful successes in their efforts. At dawn on 11 June 1944, Temporary Lieutenant Rodney Skyes RNVR, in command of MTB 448, has his boat literally ripped from under him. Having engaged a group of German E-Boats, he came under a hail of fire from a supporting German fighter; as he increased speed to get away, the damage along his waterline saw the bottom of his boat tear from under him, and MTB 448 sank. Sykes and his crew were rescued, but his accompanying press correspondent was drowned.

Overseeing all these engagements, the control officers moved between the Captain-class Frigates assigned as control ships. Each control officer was a highly experienced, battle-hardened MTB or MGB officer whose expertise, experience and stoic focus on their mission impressed everyone who encountered them. On board HMS *Stayner*, Lieutenant Ian Menzies noted for his memoirs:

> Among the control officers who had left their boats for this mission were Phillip Lee, Christopher Dreyer and Guy Hudson. All these officers, all

RNVR, had fought E-Boats throughout the entire war. They know every trick of the trade. They had suffered many casualties. They had gone back to harbour their boats riddled, their crew lying dead and wounded, and they themselves hospital cases but determinedly bringing their little boats back. They had seen their fellow officers and friends buried.[11]

With the weather providing the only respite from hostilities (when high seas across the channel prevented the small MTBs from achieving their crossing between Portsmouth and France), both the Allied and the Axis scorecards started to fill up. On the British side, MTB 632 was part of an action which sank two German R-Boat minesweepers before herself succumbing to enemy fire, and two further MTBs were lost when they rammed a German E-Boat that was trying to evade in the Seine bay. In the battle off the Channel Islands the United States lost one boat (PT 509) in an action against a German minesweeper sailing from Jersey. But, aided by a 14/15 June RAF bomber command raid on Le Havre (which damaged or destroyed about 15 E-Boats), the tide of war was by now running in favour of the Allies as German losses stacked up and their navy became increasingly fearful of sailing near the Allied patrols.

By 17 July a forward base had been opened at Arromanches and the daily routine of briefings at HMS *Hornet* or HMS *Dolphin* became intermittent. Excursions back across the channel became a rarity as the Allies consolidated their hold on their newly occupied territory with up to 27 MTBs based in France at any one time.

On 4 August 1944 the threat to the United States forces on the western flank of the landings had diminished such that two units of three US Patrol Torpedo boats were transferred to the still dangerous eastern flank. They were rapidly indoctrinated into Guy and Phillip Lee's control ship tactics and were soon to be involved in enemy action, sinking at least one enemy ship and damaging another. Simultaneously, and with the agreement of Commander-in-Chief Portsmouth together

---

[11] Ian Menzies. *We Fought Them on the Seas*. North Reading, MA: Cheshire Press, p.147.

with his US counterpart (Commander Task Force 125), it was agreed that Captain Coastal Forces Channel would relocate to Cherbourg to assist with the ongoing British battle to secure the waters around the Channel Islands.

By 5 August the first patrol was being carried out in the area, with Guy and Phillip Lee's tactics embraced by their new practitioners. A shore radio station at Jobourg (near Cap de la Hague) controlled the first mission on 5 August 1944, and by 7 August Lieutenant Commander P Scott RNVR had embarked in USS *Maloy* as the control officer.

The MTB patrols under the direction of control ships were proving to be hugely successful. Despite the novel control tactics that Guy and Phillip Lee had developed being anathema to many naval warriors of long standing, officers at all levels were embracing this new way of warfighting. Not only were MTBs listening and responding to their control radio nets, but the high quality and exceptional value of the battlefield information sent by Guy and Phillip Lee, plus their fellow SFDOs, meant that adjacent Destroyers and other ships were by now tuning in to the Coastal Forces nets in order to boost their own warfighting capability.

However, this success came at a cost, in lives. MTB engagements are by their nature close-in affairs often termed 'whites-of-the-eyes warfare'. The hail of bullets between dogfighting motor boats led to many of Guy's close comrades giving their lives for the freedom of others. This was recognised throughout the chain of command, and on 4 August a team of six medical officers was assigned for duty with the Coastal Forces. With immediate effect, one medical officer embarked in each control Frigate for their nightly patrol, with the report of their Senior Officer (Surgeon Lieutenant Commander T Ellis RNVR), embarked in HMS *Stayner*, highlighting their value:

> 8 August. A [Patrol Torpedo] boat came alongside . . . and we took off an American called Eick who had been hit by shell fragments. He had been hit high up in the thigh and in the leg. No fragments of shell could be detected within 4 inches of the wound. Bleeding was controlled and the wounds I

cleaned and dressed and Eick was put ashore . . . from our anchorage at Ryde to the [Royal Naval Hospital].

10 August. At 0300 a [Patrol Torpedo] boat with damaged steering gear was pushed alongside us by another PT. She had 2 casualties aboard. I examined these men aboard the PT. They were riddled with wounds from the waist downwards. One was shot through the eye and both had a hand each badly mutilated. They had been given their syretes of morphia and were out of pain. Field dressing had been applied but Murnick was bleeding profusely in spite of a tourniquet. The bleeding was controlled and they were transferred to our sick bay. This was all done quietly and with no fuss. The PT was put in tow. I repaired to the sick bay, where the Chief Engineer and a wardroom pantry boy proved invaluable. With complete aseptic we worked until about 0700 extracting fragments of shells which had entered at all angles, until we had quite a collection of salvage. All the wounds were dealt with individually and at 0800 when anti-gas Gangrene and AT Serum were given their conditions improved considerably. They were transferred at 0930 to a [gun boat] and taken into the Royal Naval Hospital Haslar. I had the opportunity of seeing these patients in hospital on subsequent days. They were making good progress.[12]

Surgeon Lieutenant Commander Ellis' medical report does not confine itself to the gory details of injuries sustained by those in combat. One further extract is very telling of the incredible impression made by SFDOs:

Lieutenant Lee and Lieutenant Hudson. These two young officers never relax the whole time, and have the whole game at their fingertips. The scene in the 'plot' during action and with contacts is well worth seeing.[13]

By 10 August Hudson and Lee's control ship principles had been fully grasped by their new US exponents, although much of the vectoring was

---

[12] Report on Operation Overlord – Portsmouth Command, 765/0/5, 12 September 1944 – Enclosure III (Coastal Forces), appendix 7.

[13] *Ibid.*

still being done in plain language as the US PT captains were not yet fully conversant with every aspect of the drill. Just before dawn a German convoy was detected proceeding from Guernsey to Jersey, making use of thick fog. The US PTs made three attacks, with an armed trawler identified and engaged at a range of 400 yards. At least three enemy ships were damaged by gunfire, although US PT 509 was lost in the hail of return shelling.

Three days later the British control officer was to be transferred to USS *Borum* in preparation for a more concentrated multinational patrol of the area. He hosted a meeting on board HMS *Samurez*, attended by torpedo boat commanders from the United States, Canadian, Free French and Royal Navies. Within two hours of the participants dispersing, they were in action against the enemy, with radar-assisted vectoring sending multiple units into the fight 'without risk of confusion or misidentification'.[14] Hudson and Lee's tactics continued to be adopted ever more widely.

With German forces increasingly on the defensive, the MTBs under their control ships were ready for the final phase of this battle: the defeat of German forces in Le Havre. Nightly patrols, carefully coordinated to deliver the highest practicable levels of firepower against the enemy, were arranged at the daily briefings. But with the risk of fratricide an ever-present thorn floating on the congested sea, the SFDOs could not relax. Night after night, Guy and his fellow SFDOs coordinated multiple battles attritting the enemy and driving them ever further from the precious landing beachheads.

For his part in attacks mounted on German forces as they evacuated Le Havre by sea from 23 to 28 August, Guy was nominated for the DSC. Guy's nomination stated that:

> During the evacuation of Le Havre this officer acted as a controller on five out of the seven nights. The frigates in which he was embarked were

---

[14] Report on Operation Overlord – Portsmouth Command, 765/0/5, 12 September 1944 – Enclosure III (Coastal Forces), Part II, para. 103.

frequently under heavy and prolonged fire from shore batteries.

As the pioneer, with Lieutenant Lee, in the control ship technique, he has acted as a controller on 45 nights since 5th June 1944.

He has shown himself skilful and courageous and a sound tactician, and has been tireless in his devotion to duty and determination.

Signed: Patrick V M McLaughlin, Captain Royal Navy, Captain Coastal Forces, Channel

On 14 December 1944, Temporary Lieutenant Richard Guy Ormonde Hudson, Royal Naval Volunteer Reserve, was awarded the Distinguished Service Cross. This was announced in the supplement to the *London Gazette* dated 14 November 1944, at page 5226.

With Normandy secure, Phillip Lee was seconded to the Admiralty in London whilst Guy and Fison were despatched to translate their tactics to the Nore Command (based at Dover), this time with a focus on cooperation between surface forces and aircraft. Joining HMS *Beehive* on 23 October 1944, they worked out of RAF Langham in Norfolk, where they refined control techniques for radar-equipped Wellington aircraft of 16 Group. These aircraft had been fitted with very high frequency radio to talk directly with surface forces and could direct Destroyers and Frigates to engage German minelaying vessels attempting to resow mines in British-swept channels. Given appropriate vectoring information, they could also direct MTB strike forces to intercept enemy patrols.

Operations in the Nore Command had identified that the Germans were using GSR radar intercept equipment to recognise when they were being tracked and closed by surface ships. Orders within the Nore area (which included the Dover Strait and southern North Sea) therefore restricted the use by Motor Torpedo Boats of their radar equipment. The provision by aircraft of bearing and intercept information, derived by accurate identification and plotting of both British and enemy forces, thus proved to be of considerable benefit when closing the enemy for a surprise attack.

The tactic proved to be very successful. Indeed, on the very first night it was tried in anger it proved to be too successful, when the British Motor Torpedo Boat receiving intercept vector information 'relying solely on the ranges and bearings signalled on R/T by the aircraft . . . on a dark night . . . resulted in the collision, to our disadvantage, between the MTBs and the E-Boats'. This outcome was classed as 'an expensive victory for the [British] MTBs'.[15]

Having successfully translated his control and interception methods from surface ships to the world of air–maritime cooperation, on 22 November 1944 Guy joined the Royal Navy's navigation school at HMS *Dryad*. Five miles north of Portsmouth, this was a truly wonderful place to work. Very close to the headquarters of Captain Coastal Forces on the hill at Ports-down, the Southwark Park estate and manor house were exceptionally grand and far detached from the requisitioned boarding houses, holiday camps and theatres Guy had been used to.

The high-ceilinged 'map room' in Southwark Park house had been the nerve centre of the D-Day landings. General Eisenhower had directed the invasion from this very location until he had moved his headquarters to France. And now it was to be Guy's place of work until the end of the war. The main house even had an absolutely wonderful croquet lawn on its sunny southern side, bringing back memories of trays of gin and tonic placed at either end of his grandfather's croquet court down in Devon. Guy's pace of life in the war adjusted accordingly.

Six weeks later, on 6 January 1945, and attended by his very close friend Lieutenant Phillip Lee RNVR, Guy married Sylvia in the King's Chapel of the Savoy in Savoy Hill, London, which as the chapel of the Royal Victorian Order was a beautiful 16th century church, originally built with monies bequeathed by King Henry VII.

---

[15] *Coastal Forces Periodic Review*, March–June 1945, p.49.

Theirs was a wedding typical of wartime; Sylvia listed her address as 15 Savoy Street, which was in fact a tavern on an adjacent road and which is repeatedly listed as an abode in the chapel's register of marriages due to its willingness to provide accommodation for brides wishing to marry their beaus before they went back to war. This wartime service was provided by the resident clergy, Reverend Williams, who was a very progressive chaplain renowned for doing everything he could to help warfighting members of the armed forces to marry with the least practicable inconvenience.

Sylvia Mary Price was the elder daughter of Major Hubert Davenport Price MC and Valentine Mary Pritchett, of Abbots Morton Manor,

Lieutenant and Mrs Guy and Sylvia Hudson, attended by Lieutenant Phillip Lee
VG private collection

Worcestershire. Her parents had married in 1918 in Kings Norton, only a few miles from Guy's family home at Middleton Hall farm, and had been blessed with their first child on 27 June 1920. Hubert Price was a very well-respected military officer, solicitor and Justice of the Peace, the son of Charles Frederick Price, also a solicitor in Kings Norton.

Hubert had served in the First World War initially as a yeoman in the Warwickshire Yeomanry, then gaining his commission on 24 August 1915 into the Staffordshire Yeomanry. He was promoted to Lieutenant with effect from 1 June 1916, six months later being seconded for duty with the Machine Gun Corps in Palestine, where on 24 August 1917 he was awarded the Military Cross 'for conspicuous Gallantry and devotion to duty. He showed the greatest courage and contempt of danger in advancing with one of his machine guns over ground swept by machine-gun and rifle fire, in order to enfilade the enemy, who were massing preparatory to attack.'[16] Hubert had returned to the Yeomanry on 27 May 1920 and resigned his commission on 18 June 1920, retaining the rank of Lieutenant. Thereafter he became a solicitor/partner at Price, Atkins and Price, and also a company director, for many years acting as the business and family solicitor for the Hudson Studios Limited and for Grandfather Richard, as well as acting throughout World War II as Commanding Officer of the Evesham Division of the Home Guard, in the rank of Major.

During the war Sylvia was working as an auxiliary nurse. She was a wonderful, charming and elegant woman, slightly more outgoing than Guy, but very much complementary to his wit and studious persona. She should also, rightly, be described as a poster-officer, having in November 1944 been selected by the Eucryl company to front a toothpaste advertising campaign. Charmed by each other, and very much in love, Guy and Sylvia made their base together in London, where Sylvia's father had extensive business interests and maintained an office and accommodation.

---

[16] *The London Gazette* Supplement 30862, 24 August 1918, p. 9916

Sylvia Price, poster girl
The Sphere, and VG private collection

Throughout the summer of 1945 Guy maintained his close connections with the Coastal Forces by spending time on the waterfront at HMS *Hornet*. Indeed, the party reputation of the Coastal Forces remained a naval legend of which Guy was determined to be a part. Buoyed by the German surrender, he was present on 22 June 1945 when his former foes drove their fearsome E-Boats across the channel and into Portsmouth harbour, berthing alongside the Gosport base to surrender both their vessels and themselves. This could have marked the true culmination of his military service, being among those to receive the broken pieces of a former enemy force, but, with war still underway in the Far East and with continued peace and stability in Europe still not guaranteed, his instructional masters continued to demand his expertise.

Guy continued to serve as a navigation instructor at HMS *Dryad* until the end of his required wartime service. As a 'hostilities only' officer, he could not be retained beyond the period of the national emergency, and he had already resumed studying for his desired career in law. Moving to London, where he and Sylvia now lived in a flat at 9a Marylebone High Street, he was released from uniformed duty on 22 May 1946. This was just in time to concentrate on the required revision for his first set of legal examinations since his time at university, six years earlier. He was successful, passing 'Trusts' with 24 marks out of 40 and, with what was later to prove considerable irony, passing 'Book Keeping' with 29 marks out of 40.

This was enough to get him back on the road to legal qualification, and straight after his formal naval discharge date of 22 July 1946 he commenced legal articles study with A J Johnson Solicitors of 6 Fitzroy Square, W1. That this was only 400 yards from his London flat was, of course, exceptionally convenient!

However, he did not lose touch with his military connections, quickly signing up to service in the Royal Naval Volunteer Service Reserve (RNVSR), which was to maintain his naval link and his sanity for a further 20 years.

AFTER ACTION

———◦◦◦———

Guy and Sylvia settled into their new life together in London. Guy had to work hard to catch up on years of legal study that had been lost to the war effort, whilst Sylvia and Guy together enjoyed the social scene of living in the capital.

In June 1948 Guy's supervisors at A J Johnson Solicitors put him forward for the final examinations to qualify as a solicitor. He did very well, passing Conveyancing, Tort, Contracts and Companies exams all with good marks. Of significance for his future, he passed the compulsory exam in Wills, Death Duties and Income Tax with a mark of 105 out of 180, and in a slightly prescient choice he also passed the optional exam in Divorce with a mark of 123 out of 180.

At the end of the summer, Guy's grandmother Annie passed away. She had been separated from Guy's grandfather for nearly 20 years, but the family was still very close. She had been living in Middleton Hall farmhouse along with two of Guy's aunts and their servants Elsie Stanford and Beatrice Williams. Although Middleton Hall was in increasing levels of disrepair, and developers were champing at the bit to continue new building in the area, Guy's aunties Kathleen and Harriet, together with their domestic staff, continued to live there for another seven years.

Having passed all the required tests, on 14 January 1949 Richard Guy Ormonde Hudson was admitted as a solicitor on the Roll of the Supreme Court, being given roll number 182974. He had qualified to practise law.

Guy secured employment with a practice at St Ives House, 18–20 High Street, Maidenhead. Working for Smallman & Son, he not only acted as a solicitor but concurrently started to specialise as a liquidator. Soon seeing this as a permanent position, in 1950 Guy and Sylvia moved to a lovely home at Fairview Cottage, Fifield, near Maidenhead. This was a delightful countrified property, surrounded by fields but with a few neighbours along one of the roadsides, which allowed them to join 'the Gin and Jag set'.

They both balanced their time between the countryside of Maidenhead and the bustle of London. Sylvia preferred London, often joining Guy when he was working from his office in town. But Guy preferred the countryside, where he could escape from the aggressive, money-focussed and cut-throat world of London law.

Guy was proving to be very successful in his chosen profession, and in May 1951 he became a partner in the solicitors Smallman & Son. He then obtained one of his biggest professional breaks through Sylvia's father, Hubert, who introduced him to Sir John Ellerman, hereditary owner of the shipping company known as 'Ellerman Lines'. Hubert Price was a gentleman of exceptional discretion who had forged considerable links with Sir John and his family, who were very private about their fortune. Sir John had in 1933 inherited a £37 million business and estate which took careful managing; lacking the business acumen of his father (also Sir John Ellerman), he engaged trusted aides to assist him. Hubert Price was at various stages the director of up to 20 companies associated with the Ellerman business, and Guy was now brought into this fold.

Sir John Ellerman (junior) had determined that on his death he wished to establish a series of trusts and foundations to benefit the arts. Guy's expertise in probate and trusts was harnessed in setting the conditions for these intentions to be fulfilled, which in 1970 would see Sir John establish the Moorgate Fund and then the New Moorgate Fund. In 1992 these merged and became the John Ellerman Foundation (as of 2017 worth over £142 million).

Guy was also maintaining his links with his former comrades at sea, participating in ongoing training as part of his duties as a Temporary Lieutenant RNVSR.

Socially, Sylvia and Guy continued to enjoy a wonderful life, including regular visits to his and her families in Birmingham, Devon and Ireland, as well as holidays abroad across Europe and beyond. Sylvia did not work, and despite trying their marriage remained childless, so she was able to join Guy for many of his excursions away from Fifield.

To be closer to Grandfather Richard, Guy's mother and father had by this time relocated to Devon, where they had purchased a small cottage, outbuilding and adjacent house at Egypt Lane in Chulmleigh. James and Doris lived in Egypt Cottage, an early 18th century 'single room' dwelling that had been merged with the outbuilding to form a largely unspoilt thatched cottage suitable for 20th century living.[17] This put James about an hour away from Guy's granddad, who was still living in Baunkyle at Seaton with his son, Richard Leigh, and his cook, Alice Claridge. Supplemented by an income from letting out half of the house adjacent to Egypt Cottage (the other half of 'Rook Park' was for use by guests), James Hudson continued to live the high life he had carved for himself using his father's fortune, and often encouraged Guy to visit and join him in indulging in a few gin and tonics to kick-start every evening. Under James' charge the family photography business of the Hudson Studios Ltd was still providing some financial support, but was now worth much less than it had been only a few decades earlier.

On 19 November 1955 Richard Hudson passed away, aged 95. Guy and Grandfather Richard had for a long time been very close (Richard had been Guy's nominated next-of-kin for much of the Second World War), and Guy was appointed in the will to be one of his executors, along with Guy's father, James, and Grandfather Richard's Birmingham-based stock-broker. Richard's estate was valued at £147,000; of this, £71,000 was paid in death duties before the residue was distributed between James, Guy, and James' two spinster sisters. Grandfather Richard's house in Seaton was passed in trust to Kathleen (Guy's Auntie Kal) and Harriet (Guy's Auntie Mardie), who quickly relocated to Devon from Middleton Hall, together with their two domestic staff. As parting recognition, and indicative of his grand lifestyle, Richard even left a severance gift of £100 for his chauffeur.

---

[17] Egypt Cottage was registered as a Grade II listed building on 25 October 1988, under English Heritage Legacy ID 97246.

Guy's share of the estate provided a very welcome boost to his and Sylvia's finances, and it was about this time that Guy started to take a much more active interest in the stock market.

As a longstanding family man, Guy wanted to see more of his relatives, but the distance between Maidenhead and Devon, where they were all now located, as well as the demands of his busy and prospering practice, prevented much travel beyond holidays. Sylvia also liked to maintain her family bonds, and Guy got on especially well with Sylvia's brother-in-law, Keith Creswell, who lived in southern Eire. Their friendship was probably aided by their shared wartime service, with Keith having been an RAF bomber pilot and Guy operating somewhat below that altitude but just as close to the enemy.

Ever the businessman, at some time in the 1950s Guy, together with Keith, developed a plan to fly smoked Irish salmon from the west coast of Ireland to England. For various reasons their plan never came to fruition; however, Keith went on to use his love of fishing to develop his idea and in the 1970s he perfected the process for smoking salmon, setting up a company to trade his innovation. Keith's son, Anthony Creswell, still runs this very successful smoked salmon business (Ummera Smoked Products) in County Cork.

Guy had also started to move into the legal area of probate, and one of his early forays into unpicking the posthumous desires of those with complex wills occurred when he was appointed executor for Leslie Gordon Courage. Leslie had joined the Royal Flying Corps in June 1916, then been commissioned into the newly formed RAF in 1918. A former RAF Flight Lieutenant who lived in Maidenhead, he passed away on 25 April 1953. Leslie had no surviving heirs and so in October Guy commenced the tortuous process of gazetting his death in order to try to find to whom his estate of £2,306 17s 6d should be disbursed.

Probate fascinated Guy, and he started to make a niche for himself in this particular field of law.

Tragically, in November 1958, Guy's father-in-law passed away, with Guy being named as an executor of Hubert Price's will. Hubert Price MC, retired solicitor, inspiration for Guy and father to his wife, was laid to rest in St Peter's Anglican Church, Abbots Morton. Building on his increasing expertise and concurrent fascination with probate and trusts, Guy was nominated as one of the trustees of Hubert's estate, taking an active part in managing the funds to the benefit of Hubert's family, including Guy's wife.

With probate, trusts and liquidation now Guy's clear field of expertise, underpinned by the minor funds he had received from his late grandfather's will, he was dabbling in the world of stocks and shares. Guy still had some friends in the fast-growing industrial metropolis of Birmingham, one of whom he referred to as 'the Mole'. During regular telephone calls, Guy's mole would pass him hints and tips on new inventions or manufacturing breakthroughs, allowing Guy to buy shares whilst they were still relatively cheap. Guy, informed by his mole, proved to be an astute judge of engineering prospects and he started to make himself some small sums of money, but not enough to live on.

Guy had become a very sweet, kind and funny husband, and uncle to Sylvia's niece and nephew. However, by this time, he was struggling to live with some of the memories he had created during the war. Using his long-standing fondness for gin and tonic, he created for himself a tipple he referred to as the 'Hudson Heart-Starter'. He often used this little brew, which was a rather strong version of a G&T, to kick-start himself at lunchtimes, or sometimes earlier.

Guy and Sylvia's marriage remained childless, which left a void in their lives; Guy wanted a family, but it was not forthcoming. Sylvia had spent many years of their marriage hiding his drinking from her relatives and the strain was beginning to show. Her family were becoming concerned for her welfare and had started to notice Guy's penchant for alcohol; he even started to mix Hudson Heart-Starters for visitors, on one occasion serving a young female guest a welcome drink of such strength that Sylvia had to put her to bed for the next hour to recover.

Guy and Sylvia Hudson
VG private collection

By this time Guy and Sylvia were, tragically, growing apart, with Guy finding solace in the self-prescribed glasses of Hudson Heart-Starter. As this spiral continued downwards he allowed his association with the Royal Naval Reserve to lapse, separating him from the camaraderie of former MTB shipmates with whom he had shared so many experiences.

In late 1969 Sylvia's mother, Valentine, passed away whilst living in London, and she was laid to rest next to her husband in her family church at Abbots Morton. Sylvia still had some links to her childhood home, but by this time very few of Guy's family lived nearby and he was hankering to move to Devon.

Things were looking bleak for Guy. He was living on the edge. He had a fast and loose lifestyle, his marriage was failing, his solicitor's practice was crumbling, he was funnelling his limited money from shares to fund his lifestyle and sinking business, his family had moved to Devon, and he was becoming (or was already) an alcoholic, unable to reconcile some of his stark wartime memories.

The situation was coming to a head, and on the evening of their silver wedding anniversary Guy and Sylvia held a family party at their London flat in Hallam Street. After reception drinks the gathering departed for their chosen restaurant, but Guy stated that he 'would catch them up'. He arrived for their meal quite a few minutes later, unsteady, 'tight' and obviously tipsy – drawing no sympathy from the male attendees but eliciting sympathy for Sylvia from her female companions. No one knew what underlay such events, and no one beyond Sylvia gave him the solace he possibly needed.

With Guy's drinking an increasingly irreconcilable problem, Sylvia was on the verge of a nervous breakdown; they decided to divorce. Concurrently, in November 1970, he dissolved the partnership at Smallman & Son, which was now almost worthless.

His ties to Maidenhead thus severed, Guy took the opportunity to relocate to Devon. His parents' Chulmleigh home being a very small cottage, he moved into their neighbouring guest accommodation – the larger half of Rook Park, with the other half of the property let out to Mr Alfred Short and his wife, both of whom were retired. This move also allowed Guy to be near to his two aunties in Seaton, less than an hour away.

But Guy's departure from Maidenhead left Sylvia without financial support; the divorce had occurred when Guy was close to penniless and there was very little to share between them. Sylvia immediately moved back into their small London flat and found work as a dental nurse, building on her wartime auxiliary experiences. She maintained links with Guy's former clients in the Ellerman family, later becoming personal assistant to Jessica de Sola, Sir John's sister-in-law.

With Guy resident in half of his parents' spare property he too needed an income. In January 1971 he registered to practise as an independent solicitor. He also started to take care of his parents, including regular visits to collect their prescriptions from the local doctor, where he made the acquaintance of the head medical receptionist, Patricia Wright. Patricia, or Pat (as she was known), had been born Patricia Jesse Rowland-Hill on 28 December 1918 in Sussex. After marrying in 1942, she had worked in a shop in Maidstone. But her marriage did not last and she soon divorced her husband Robert before moving away to Devon, still under her married name. Pat was to become a key figure in Guy's life, but not until after he had fallen at the next hurdle.

Guy's independent legal practice suffered from maladministration and, although he managed to maintain a steady client base as well as securing locum work with local legal firms, he was soon under investigation. On 5 April 1972 the accounting year ended for his first full year of independent practice. He had until 5 October 1972 to submit his accounts to the Law Society, but he failed to do so.

On 19 June 1973 a Mr Gallacher, assistant to Mr Harold Greenhalgh (the Law Society's investigative accountant), attended Guy's office in Chulmleigh. Guy told Mr Gallacher that he was conducting a small general practice without assistance of any staff, that he was not a solicitor-trustee, and that he was unable to produce any bank statements later than December 1971. The local Lloyds bank did, however, certify that he had £6,533.08 in a 'client account' and £849.81 in an 'office account'. Of key significance was the fact that the investigator was unable to determine if Guy had sufficient funds to cover his liability to clients, some of whom had made deposits in anticipation of future transactions. Six weeks later, on 2 August 1973, an application was made by the investigating solicitors that Richard Guy Ormonde Hudson of Rook Park, Chulmleigh, answer formal allegations of lack of accounts-keeping.

This troublesome period was accentuated by Guy's further descent into alcoholism, attributable to the death of his aunt Harriet on 11 August 1973. Harriet was living at Baunkyle in Seaton, Guy's grandfather's former house. Both Harriet and Auntie Kathleen were spinsters who had been living a 1920s lifestyle, and their domestic staff were also ageing fast.

Guy, who was suffering such turmoil in his own life, now also needed to divert increasing levels of attention to looking after his parents, with whom he shared a house, and his surviving auntie.

Whilst Guy was integrating with his family in Devon, he was resisting breaking ties with his former family. Having been nominated as a trustee in the will of Hubert Price, Sylvia's father, he continued to undertake this duty, for which he received a useful stipend. Not surprisingly, Sylvia and her family no longer wished her estranged husband to be intimately involved with managing their money, but Guy was reluctant to cut off one of his sources of income. Confronted by a rising number of key trust decisions requiring settlement, and under pressure from his former in-laws, Guy eventually stood aside, striking out his last ties to the Price clan.

Concurrently, on 21 December 1973 a disciplinary hearing was held at the Law Society. Guy did not attend, but in his absence it was found that the allegations of lack of accounts-keeping were substantiated. He would be struck off the roll of solicitors.

Much to Guy's embarrassment, this was immediately reported in his local newspaper (the *North Devon Journal-Herald*), followed on 3 January 1974 by the following official notice appearing in the *London Gazette*:

In the Matter of the Solicitors Act 1957

Notice is hereby given, pursuant to section 49(3) of the Solicitors Act 1957, that on the 21st December 1973, an Order was made by the Disciplinary Committee constituted under the Solicitors Act 1957, that the name of Richard Guy Ormonde Hudson, of Rook Park, Egypt Lane, Chulmleigh, Devon, be struck off the Roll of Solicitors of the Supreme Court, and that he do pay the applicant his costs of and incidental to the application and enquiry, such costs to be taxed by one of the Taxing Masters of the Supreme Court – Dated 21st December 1973.

[Signed] H Horsfall Turner, Secretary, The Law Society

Guy was no longer legally allowed to practise law.

Wedded to his Hudson Heart-Starters, Guy needed something or someone to get him out of his spiral of despair. He started to talk more and more with Pat, who was also somewhat lonely, following the departure of her adult daughter to South Africa. Their friendship blossomed; Pat stepped into the breach and started the long process of weaning him off the bottle. Once they started to get to know each other properly, rather than as acquaintances at medical reception, they quickly fell for each other, and a few months later, in June 1974, they were married.

Guy moved out of his parents' second house and into Pat's terraced home at Mole Hill, New Street, in Chulmleigh. Pat was the breadwinner, and Guy felt a patriarchal responsibility to contribute to their new family income.

Guy's brilliance at probate and trusts enabled him to find some work for a local firm of solicitors, Chanter, Burrington & Foster, of Bridge Chambers in Barnstaple. One of the senior partners then introduced Guy to a talented stockbroker, Mr Christopher Corfield, which was to prove of significant benefit in Guy's long-term financial success. Christopher had served as a territorial solider in the Honourable Artillery Company, so he shared much of Guy's military sense of humour, and they got on well. Less appreciated was Christopher's introduction to Guy's Hudson Heart-Starter, which proved especially intoxicating when trying to discuss details of finance. Christopher quickly realised that the Hudson Heart-Starter, along with Guy's other alcoholic vices, could be Guy's downfall, and thus resolved to drink with Guy only when Pat was present to manage the fallout.

A year into their marriage, Pat became increasingly anxious about Guy's drinking and worked with his doctor to encourage him to go to Alcoholics Anonymous. However, sitting in groups with people he did not know was an anathema to Guy and he resisted their persuasion.

Just after Pat's daughter Sally returned from South Africa, Pat persuaded Guy to return to the doctor, where he opened up about his drinking habit and was prescribed 'Antabuse', otherwise known as disulfiram, which is used in the treatment of alcoholism. This drug quickly became a key element in Guy's life as he daily mustered the willpower to stay away from alcohol; if someone who has taken Antabuse subsequently drinks alcohol, they suffer what is best described as an allergic reaction and very quickly vomit. It is very effective, but only when combined with the willpower to both stay away from alcohol and take this medication on a daily basis.

Inspired by Pat's love for him, and her desire for him to stop drinking, Guy abruptly ceased all alcohol. As was to be expected, he rapidly descended into the DTs, or delirium tremens, which saw him undergo violent mood swings as well as the 'shakes' which can be a side effect of coming off a powerful drug. But the end goal of sobriety was worth the effort and, encouraged by Pat and the Damoclean sword of Antabuse, he stuck to his zero-alcohol regime.

Guy was by now proving to be a successful investor. Acting on the intelligence he received from 'the Mole', together with his still acute sense of business honed through his legal work, he made enough money to build a quite diverse and very successful portfolio of shares centred on the British engineering industry. He was making considerable sums of money, which he perpetuated through extreme diligence in trading and understanding of the stock market. Guy was by now quite obsessive, and he liked strict routine. He would every day study the financial pages of the newspapers in order to ensure he was wholly up-to-date on the latest business and engineering opportunities, telephoning his stockbroker whenever he could make a good deal.

In a further transition back towards normality he focussed his renewed energy on resuming his legal career. Under the loving inspiration of Pat, he studied for and resat his legal exams, achieving huge personal success when he was readmitted to the Roll of the Supreme Court (with the same roll number). He also resumed a more normal social life, occasionally inviting around his auntie from Seaton, but never at the same time as his half-uncle Richard, who both aunties had refused to accept into the family.

Guy and Pat now lived a settled and happy life that was almost entirely alcohol-free. Guy remained very reticent about the war but seemed to be coping within himself, containing his memories of fighting the Axis enemy and the consequences of battle. He was charmingly focussed about a few things, including his strict adherence to routines; Wednesday was for shopping in Exeter (at Marks and Spencer, in which he had invested), the morning was for reading (in huge detail) the day's newspapers, and he had an immaculate collection of paperweights on which he was increasingly expert.

Working with Christopher Corfield, often after a tip from 'the Mole', Guy massaged his shares portfolio to grow very considerably. Acting on an interesting mixture of intelligence, instinct and acumen, when he spotted investment opportunities he would instruct Christopher, often by letter or increasingly by telephone, on buying and selling his shares. Dovetailing this with his extensive portfolio of managing probate and trusts at what was now Chanter Ferguson Solicitors (following a merger), Guy had once again become financially secure.

The first two years of the 1980s proved testing. Guy's parents' health was failing, so he arranged for them to live in a rather lovely residential home in nearby Crediton. His auntie Kathleen also needed increasing levels of care but was too far away in Seaton for Guy to provide this, so she moved closer to Chulmleigh and lived at the Heathermoor Nursing Home in Barnstaple. Sadly, his mother Doris – known to everyone as Polly – passed away on 6 May 1980. Only nine months later, Auntie Kathleen passed on 7 February 1981, followed devastatingly quickly by Guy's father James, who died on 7 March 1981. The family expert on probate, Guy was the executor for all of their wills, with James' will being especially complex as, after the sale of Egypt Cottage, it left all of the £128,000 that remained of the family fortune to his wife, who had pre-deceased him.

With huge support from Pat and her daughter Sally, Guy got through this period and continued to both practise law and make considerable sums on the stock market, using the legacy monies from his relatives to boost his portfolio. He also became good friends with his own family solicitor, Jeremy Lee, who worked with Christopher Corfield's friend, Arthur Robinson, at Symes Robinson & Lee Solicitors. These friends, together with his wonderful wife, soon helped Guy to resume the happy life he had been living since his second marriage.

By now Guy wanted to spend more time with Pat and their two beagles, Basil and Jezebel, and so he wound down his legal duties and in 1982 retired from Chanter's practice.

Having sold Guy's parents' former home at Egypt Cottage, Guy and Pat still derived a small income from the letting of half the adjacent cottage, Rook Park. The tenant, Alfred Short, was 78 and lived a quiet life with his wife Olive; Alfred passed away in early 1982 whilst tending his vegetable patch, and Olive soon moved out to avoid living in an old property on a steep lane. This presented Guy and Pat with an opportunity to redevelop Rook Park into their dream retirement home, which they commenced with a wonderful shared passion. They knocked through the cottage to convert it from two separate dwellings into one, set about landscaping the gardens to include fountains, a fish pond and nesting boxes to support Guy's passion for ornithology, and were soon able to move out of Pat's home at Mole Hill and into their own countrified cottage.

Guy was enormously happy in his retirement, living with nature, a wonderful wife and their two dogs. When Basil and Jezebel passed away from old age they found two more beagle puppies which they named Castor and Pollux, testament either to the Greek gods who are together known as the patrons of sailors, or simply to two of the bright stars Guy had tracked with a traditional sextant when navigating his MTBs.

Gently growing older, Guy formally retired on 31 January 1990 when his name was removed from the solicitors' roll. At this dawn of the internet age, he was also increasingly unable to keep up with the required pace of stock market transactions, preferring voice-telephone to modem, so he concurrently divested much of his portfolio into less dynamic investments.

Particularly aware of his own mortality due to many years of heavy drinking, Guy started to settle his financial affairs, and on 11 November 1991 he signed a will drawn up for him by his friend Jeremy Lee. Being childless, Guy wished to ensure first and foremost that Pat was looked after, and thus he detailed his posthumous trust that would ensure her financial security. He also wished to ensure that Pat's daughter, Sally, was left in a comfortable situation; Sally lived nearby and she, with her two children, visited often to enjoy family time with Guy and Pat.

Guy's luck with money contrasted with his private life, and in 1991 Pat became ill with a kidney infection. Despite her having worked for much of her life in the local doctor's surgery, for three years they dismissed many of her complaints before a locum spotted some subtle symptoms and changed her treatment. However, following a tragic series of mini-strokes, Pat passed away on 1 December 1994.

The dark side of Guy's life crash-started again. He very quickly stopped taking his Antabuse and recommenced drinking — heavily. Pat had been his rock for the last 20 years, but without her he was unable to keep suppressed the haunting memories that were still raw in his mind, despite 50 years of peaceful life as a civilian. During the war he had twice seen shipmates drown only yards from being rescued; he had been unable to fight for his former Destroyer shipmates as they were pummelled by Axis guns; he had helped ships discharge their dead after combat, the memory accentuated by those who had been gunned down being his close friends and colleagues; and he had endured repeated funerals of professional peers succumbing to enemy fire as they defended the freedom and democracy of the country he held so very dear.

Guy wished to keep this demon from his friends, and so he kept visiting the doctor's surgery to collect his prescription, he kept visiting the pharmacist to collect his drugs, and he simply deposited the vital Antabuse pills in his garden shed, hiding them among the increasing numbers of empty alcohol bottles he would not throw away in the rubbish. His stepdaughter, Sally, became suspicious after a number of strange telephone calls at increasingly odd hours, but she was unable to break into his mind, which was by now overcome by the demons Pat had for 20 years helped to suppress.

Sending Christmas cards was a painful experience, contacting friends and acquaintances to let them know that what for them was a season of happiness would, for Guy, be incredibly sad. He received many responses, including one from a former client, and gin-and-jag socialite, called Marion, who was living in London. With contact made, and with Guy living a very lonely life consoled mainly by alcohol, Marion quickly became a friend, and the friend quickly became a regular visitor. Guy's closest friends tried to warn him that his new companion appeared motivated by money and not Guy's best interests, but the apparent sunshine of a new single female companion may have clouded Guy's judgement.

After ascertaining that Guy had amassed a small fortune to support his comfortable lifestyle, his new companion tried to influence him to change his will, or alternately to get married (which in UK law automatically annuls all previous wills in favour of the new spouse), or both. Again, Guy's friends counselled him against such a course of action, citing his new friend's apparent dislike of Guy's wishes to bequeath much of his money to charity.

Marion introduced Guy to her personal solicitors at Gray's Inn Square, who helped Guy draw up a new will, which was due to be signed on 29 June 1995. However, despite his new happiness with Marion, Guy was increasingly consumed by the demon of drink and the week before he was to travel to Marion's solicitors he sought solace by calling his first wife, Sylvia. She took his call, they spoke for a while, but after years of almost no contact there was little that could be achieved in one conversation. Sylvia still had feelings for Guy, but tragedy was to intervene.

On 26 June 1995 Guy and Marion were having dinner together, lounging in front of the television at Rook Park. Without the deterrent of Antabuse, Guy had re-found his penchant for a regular Hudson Heart-Starter and often accompanied his meals with a drink, or two, or a few. This evening was no exception. Whilst he was still eating his main course Marion went to the kitchen; with sounds of choking coming from the lounge, Marion raced to see what had happened, but Guy had suffocated due to his airway being blocked by a piece of meat. An ambulance was called, but there was nothing that could be done for him.

At an inquest held in Barnstaple in early August 1995, the pathologist remarked that 'choking on large portions of unchewed food which entered the larynx occasionally occurred in diners with high blood-alcohol levels';[18] despite it being quite early in the evening, Guy's blood alcohol levels were already three times the legal drink-drive limit.

Patricia's daughter, Sally, was Guy's nearest living relative and was immediately called to the house. Only seven months after losing her mother, Sally had lost a dear stepfather. Her pain was accentuated by the unusual circumstances of Guy's death, which required formal investigation, resulting in a verdict of accidental death. Sally also had to clear out Rook Park, and when she entered his garden shed her worst fears were realised; hidden among Wellington boots, fishing rods and empty bottles of wine was six months' supply of Antabuse.

Marion was also still there, aware of the full consequences of Guy's still extant will. She asserted that Guy had proposed marriage, that their meal was to celebrate their engagement, and thus she should be brought into the beneficiary fold, but Sally stood her ground. Marion also produced a letter purportedly from Guy asking her to take 24 of his expensive French paperweights to Sotheby's Auction House in London in order to have them valued. She then packed her things, packed most of Guy's extensive collection of valuable paperweights (using the letter as an attestation of ownership), and departed with the remark, 'All that business of leaving money to charity, I don't agree with it'.

Sally, along with Jeremy Lee and Guy's stockbroker Christopher, was assigned as an executor of his will. Guy had been survived by his first wife Sylvia, who was living in Collingwood Square, London, still under her married name. She later passed away on 6 October 1999, having finally had her financial woes addressed through a bequest from a former employer left to her in 1994.

---

[18] *North Devon Journal*, 10 August 1995, p.7

HUDSON'S LEGACY

—⋅⊸⊙⊶⋅—

With the dust settled on the unusual circumstances of Guy's death, his friends had to face the task of enacting his last wishes. His long-standing family solicitor held a will signed in November 1991 in which Guy intended to create a trust for his beloved second wife, Patricia, ensuring she would benefit from their fortune for as long as she lived. However, Patricia had pre-deceased Guy, so the other provisions of the will would by default become active, distributing the bulk of his assets to charity. His recently renewed friendship with former client Marion saw her assert that Guy was about to update his will 'in contemplation of marriage' (to her), which in English law would allow a new will not only to override immediately his previous charitable distributions but also to remain extant after any subsequent wedding to her. Extensive searches were made by his family solicitor, an unsigned document was found, and an appropriate amount of time was duly allowed for challenges against his signed will. However, and despite newspaper articles of both his death and the subsequent inquest, no valid alternate document was presented and no challenge made. Thus, his last will and testament was deemed to be that signed on 11 November 1991.

Probate was obtained on 12 October 1995. Despite being almost destitute in 1970 when he was divorced, by 1995 he had amassed a fortune of £1,558,124. However, Patricia's pre-deceasing of Guy meant that the will would require some careful legal unpicking; Guy's now absent expertise at probate of such matters drew many a wry smile.

Some of his assets were bequeathed as specific legacies, including his great-great-grandfather's Waterloo Medal, which was given to the Birmingham Municipal Museum (where it still resides), and his favourite oil painting, by Daniel Cobb, of HMS *Sikh* attacking the German battleship *Bismarck* being left to the National Maritime Museum for loan to the officers' mess at HMS *Dryad*, where he had taught navigation. The museum turned down the kind bequest, as it already had too many pictures of that genre, and so it hung for the next ten years at HMS *Dryad* on direct loan from the trustees before that establishment was closed by the shrinking Royal Navy.

Guy's financial assets were considerable, and after liquidation by his executors they were divided into three equal shares. His will specified their distribution:

> as to one such share upon trust absolutely for the Chancellor Masters and Scholars of the University of Oxford and I express the wish that this bequest be utilised to fund the further education of Officers of the Royal Navy or Royal Marines at the University.

> as to one such share upon trust absolutely for the Royal National Lifeboat Institution of West Quay Road, Poole, Dorset, BH15 1HZ.

> as to one such share upon trust absolutely for the Imperial Cancer Research Fund of PO Box 123, Lincoln's Inn Fields, London, WC2A 3PX.

Each share was worth half a million pounds. The shares for the Lifeboat and the Cancer Research fund were relatively simple to transact, each being taken into the general funds of the respective organisation for spending as it saw fit. The other share proved to be somewhat more interesting to execute while ensuring Guy's wishes were fully considered.

Before he died, Guy had discussed his will with his stepdaughter Sally, who was one of his executors. He had wanted to leave some money to the Royal Navy due to his perception that there was an increasing lack of funding for his former service, and there was a particular lack of finance for the training of good naval officers. Sally's recollection of his intentions gave the executors a wonderful baseline from which to develop his long-term legacy.

The trustees, led by former Royal Marine turned solicitor Jeremy Lee, approached Captain Peter Hore Royal Navy, who was at that time the Royal Navy's Head of Defence Studies. Together they approached the University of Oxford's development office, which was very willing to accept and administer the bequest, but the percentage fee it quoted by way of office administration costs horrified the executors. Everyone agreed that the terms of the bequest were sufficiently broad to give some latitude in managing the funds when seeking to educate naval service personnel at the university and that it was undesirable for Guy's generous gift to be gradually negated by administration fees. A more subtle approach was thus required.

Captain Hore sought advice from Professor Bob O'Neill, who was at the time a fellow at All Souls College (University of Oxford), the Chichele Professor of the History of War, and the chairman of the university's Delegacy for Military Instruction. They discussed a model for optimising the benefit from Guy's bequest, which centred on a rather successful excursion into academia by Admiral Sir James Eberle GCB.

'Jim' Eberle, as he was affectionately known, had built for himself a reputation as a highly literate sailor. Educated at Clifton College, Bristol, he had joined the Royal Navy in September 1944, serving initially in Motor Torpedo Boats before joining HM Ships *Renown* and *Belfast* during the last year of the war. A gunnery specialist, he went on to command HMS *Intrepid*. Shortly after promotion to flag rank in 1971, he had turned down a place at the Ministry of Defence's Royal College of Defence Studies (RCDS), instead researching at University College, University of Oxford. This period of study allowed him to contribute major sections to *Management in the Armed Forces: An Anatomy of the Military Profession*, edited by John Downey and published by McGraw-Hill in 1977. His rise to prominence as Commander-in-Chief Fleet, then as Commander-in-Chief Naval Home Command, had been meteoric, and it was believed by many in the Royal Navy that this could, in part, be attributed to his academic success at Oxford as well as his prowess whilst at the NATO Staff Defence College and other intellectually broadening assignments. The aspiration for Guy's legacy thus became to replicate the opportunity for relatively senior Royal Navy and Royal Marines officers to study at the university and to use their newly acquired breadth of academic enquiry for the benefit of the navy and the nation.

Professor O'Neill seized upon this idea of establishing an alternative to RCDS for high fliers who were able to conduct their own research without supervision, and he 'made a few telephone calls'. His own college, All Souls, was very exclusive in both its methods of selection and its modus of tenure, so he used his connections to determine that the all-graduate college of St Antony's had developed a particularly good programme for visiting fellows. This was exactly the opportunity both the Royal Navy and the executors had in mind, and in response to a motion proposed by Professor Archie Brown the governing body of St Antony's College agreed to act as primary host, noting that 'the Fellowship is intended for members of the Royal Navy, expected to reach senior positions, to be attached to the College for a year at a time as a Visiting Fellow in order to study international relations and related subjects'.

Professor O'Neill formed a committee of trustees to administer the financial aspects of the legacy, who would also guide the anticipated cohort of naval officers, some of whom had never been to university, through the mazes that are Oxford traditions, customs and bureaucracy. The committee was led by Professor Christopher Davis, a former Lieutenant in the United States Navy and graduate of Harvard, George Washington and Cambridge Universities, who was at the time a governing body fellow at Wolfson College. Under his chairmanship the Guy Hudson Memorial Fund was thus founded on 22 September 1997, by decree of the University of Oxford's Hebdomadal Council:

> The University accepts with gratitude the bequest by the late Mr Richard Guy Ormonde Hudson, DSC, of one-third of the residue of his estate to establish a fund to be known as the Guy Hudson Memorial Fund, the net income from which shall be used for the education of officers of the Royal Navy or Royal Marines at the University.

After receiving nominations for three naval candidates, St Antony's College accepted Captain (later Commodore) Guy Challands Royal Navy as the first 'Hudson Fellow'. As well as sharing his benefactor's moniker, Captain Challands shared Guy's concerns regarding funding levels for the Royal Navy. His research between October 1997 and September 1998 centred on developing a thesis titled 'Sense about European Defence: Affordable arms procurement through collaboration?' to argue against the commonly held view that European collaboration in procurement of major defence projects is economical, is timely and delivers interoperability.

Guided by Professor O'Neill, Captain Challands concurrently set about establishing a lasting legacy at the university for both Guy and the Royal Navy. As well as attending numerous lectures, courses and seminars, he participated in the student-led Oxford University Strategic Studies Group – a connection that endures today. He also invited numerous senior naval officers to the university to meet and dine with Oxford's senior academic staff, thus broadening the academic benefit beyond just the incumbent Hudson Fellow by facilitating the attendance, albeit overnight, of many other Royal Navy and Royal Marines officers.

Over the course of the first few years the trustees established a firm foundation for the longevity of the fund by focussing the disbursement of income generated by Guy's bequest on the provision of a fellowship for a senior Royal Navy or Royal Marines Officer to study at Oxford. Beyond this headline commitment, it was identified that in due course Guy's generous bequest could also support more junior officers in their studies (as a 'Junior Hudson Fellow'), as well as pay for legal courses for Royal Navy or Royal Marines lawyers undertaking advanced short-course studies.

In the autumn of 1997 Commodore (later Vice Admiral) Tim Laurence MVO was awarded the Hudson Fellowship. Again elected as a Visiting Research Fellow by St Antony's College, he integrated with the International Studies department under Professor Adam Roberts whilst being mentored by Professor O'Neill.

The United Kingdom was part of the endgame of the Kosovo crisis, and between January and June 1998 Commodore Laurence developed a thesis on 'Peacekeeping and Humanitarian Assistance – an uneasy alliance?' The Warden of St Antony's, Sir Marrack Goulding, was a former Head of Peacekeeping at the United Nations and rapidly became an invaluable co-mentor, with Commodore Laurence's paper later published by the Royal United Services Institute as a great descriptor of some principles guiding relations between peacekeepers and humanitarians when they are deployed together.

The trustees of the Guy Hudson Memorial Fund had by this time generated a sustainable income of about £14,000 per year, allowing some limited additional disbursements. The Commanding Officer of the Oxford University Royal Naval Unit (URNU) had been co-opted as the secretary to the trustees, and in an effort to widen the list of beneficiaries he developed some bids for more junior personnel. One early bid, which was approved, was to support an URNU Midshipman studying physiotherapy at Oxford Brookes University, leading to the fund purchasing a portable treatment table for her. Such disbursement established the principle that the URNU officers could equally benefit from the fund, provided that it remained sustainable in the long term. Annual grants were also established for the purchase of naval books for the Codrington Library at All Souls College and a grant to the especially informative Oxford University Strategic Studies Group, to which all Hudson Fellows were becoming affiliated.

The next Hudson Fellow was Captain Graham Wiltshire Royal Navy, who had returned to the UK after serving as the Naval Attaché in Rome. As a Visiting Research Fellow at St Antony's College his enquiry centred on 'Military Intervention in the Post-Cold War Era: The Western way of warfare under stress'. After a year of research combined with enhancing the Royal Navy's reputation among Oxford academics and visiting scholars, Captain Wiltshire found himself up against a deadline to deliver his final paper. In torrential rain reminiscent of some of the storms faced by Guy in his MTB, Captain Wiltshire spent his last night in Oxford cycling around various colleges to deliver his thesis to his various mentors; early the following morning he departed on a flight to Australia, where he had been assigned as the UK's Defence Advisor to Canberra, receiving one especially lovely comment on his output which asserted that that 'any paper that cites Edward Gibbon is likely to be a good read'.

The successful investment strategy of the trustees had by this time generated sufficient income to allow a 'Junior' Hudson Fellow to benefit from Guy's legacy. Commander Charles Ashcroft Royal Navy was thus awarded a Junior Hudson Fellowship to study for a year at Christ Church, undertaking a programme more akin to an undergraduate timetable of formalised lectures, essays and tutorials. This cost the fund about £5,000, but the status of the junior fellow within his college, where he was treated as a visiting undergraduate rather than as a senior Royal Navy Officer, caused some concerns. This was accentuated in Trinity term when the needs of the armed forces led to the Royal Navy withdrawing him just before the end of his formalised studies. Commander Ashcroft was to be the only fellow to undertake such a structured programme, all subsequent attendees being focussed instead on original maritime and military research.

The Hudson Fellowship had by this time gained considerable kudos, including attracting the attention of the United States Navy. During his wartime service Guy had built some strong affiliations with the US Navy, including during his operations out of Sousse when the US Patrol Torpedo boat 203 had been instrumental in rescuing his friends from MTB 61 after it ran aground under the Axis fort at Kelibia, and also in 1944 when the US enthusiastically embraced his surface force direction tactics. In a wonderfully apposite move, the US Navy wrote to the University of Oxford requesting permission to use the title 'Hudson Fellow' for members of the Navy's Federal Executive Programme who attended the university. After some deliberations surrounding the terms of Guy's bequest it was agreed that whilst the Hudson Fund could not provide any financial support to the US Fellow (the costs of the US fellowship being borne by their government), it would be a positive development of the fellowship for Guy's name to also be taken by the US Navy nominee.

The United States Navy then entered a direct arrangement with St Antony's College whereby the navy would nominate three candidates, from whom the college would select one Visiting Research Fellow who would be known as the 'US Navy Hudson Fellow'. The inaugural US Hudson Fellow, arriving in September 2000, was Commodore Kenneth Golden USN. He researched on possible conflict between the United States and the People's Republic of China over the island nation of Taiwan, as well as establishing for the United States a formidable reputation for the rigour of their fellowship.

The next 'senior' Royal Navy Hudson Fellow was Commander (later Professor) Steven Haines Royal Navy. In January 2001 he joined St Antony's College to research the law of military operations. His fellowship included some unusual avenues of research when out of term time he deployed throughout the summer at NATO's Multinational Brigade headquarters in Pristina (Kosovo), followed by a further out-of-term research trip to the United Kingdom's Joint Task Force Headquarters in Sierra Leone. Both of these locations were active military theatres of operations, where Commander Haines was able both to advance his studies and to give operational legal advice to his hosts. Taken together, these deployments make Commander Haines the only incumbent to have earned two operational campaign medals during their time as Hudson Fellow.

By the end of his fellowship in December 2001 Commander Haines had completed the drafting of the 2001 edition of British Defence Doctrine and had progressed the drafting of the maritime chapter of the United Kingdom's Manual on the Law of Armed Conflict. Using his new contacts from the University of Oxford he continued to work on this manual after his fellowship was completed, returning to St Antony's College in 2004 for the manual's formal launch by the then Attorney General, Lord Goldsmith.

Following the 2001 handover by Professor O'Neill as Chichele Professor of the History of War to Professor (later Sir) Hew Strachan (like Guy, a former Rugbeian), the trustees investigated adjusting the nature of the programme to give Hudson Fellows a formal qualification. However, it was determined that the full costs of such a venture as well as the occasionally dynamic nature of Royal Navy attendance (exemplified by Commander Ashcroft's experience) would make such a move financially difficult to sustain. The efficacy of this decision was proved almost straight away when the 2001 Royal Navy Hudson Fellow, Commodore (later Rear Admiral) Neil Latham, had for service reasons to postpone commencement of his attendance at St Antony's College until January 2002. Upon his arrival, his enquiries focussed on globalisation and the defence industry, and he was published by the Royal United Services Institute (RUSI) as part of their Whitehall Paper series.

In the summer of 2002 Commander (later Commodore) Nick Roberts was elected as the Royal Navy Hudson Fellow. His preparation for the fellowship had been somewhat unusual as whilst practising delivery of his research proposal, scheduled for 12 September 2001, he had watched with the rest of the world the awful 9/11 attacks in the USA. Having been given an additional week to (re)shape his thoughts, his research morphed to look at the strategic implications of the international community's emerging campaign against global reach terrorism.

With operations in Afghanistan and controversy surrounding the invasion of Iraq providing the strategic backdrop, debate in seminars, conferences, studies and bars across Oxford was lively, polarised and constantly challenging. Notwithstanding all this discourse, Commander Roberts' research was being hindered as there was no generally accepted definition of terrorism. Thus the Hudson Fellow produced his own; 'Defining Global Reach Terrorism' was published in the *Journal of Defence Studies* and was also presented to the Oxford University Strategic Studies Group in All Souls College.

From these rather esoteric beginnings, Commander Roberts focussed on the strategic challenges facing the international community in its attempts to frame a coherent international counter-terrorist policy and in particular the systemic, legal and ethical limitations of the use of force. The ensuing short paper, entitled 'Some Limitations of Consensus on the Campaign Against Global Reach Terrorism', was presented to the Central European Academy of Science and Arts' International Congress on the New Peace Architecture in Băile Herculane, Romania, and was published in the congress proceedings.

The theme of a changed world order was pursued by the 2003 Royal Navy Hudson Fellow, with Commander Mike Mason later publishing his thesis on homeland security in the *RUSI Journal*. 2003 also saw publication of a suite of fellowship research with the inaugural 'Hudson Papers'. Five hundred copies were printed, containing Commander Roberts' 'Countering Global Reach Terrorism: Limitations of the use of military force' alongside the final theses of Commodore Latham and Commander Haines, with printing costs borne by the Hudson Trust (as it had become known).

The year 2003 also saw the founding in the university of the Changing Character of War (CCW) programme, dedicated to bringing together scholars and practitioners to investigate how war and armed conflict is morphing through time. The Hudson Trust was approached to affiliate with CCW, both through Hudson Fellows being accredited to the CCW programme and through small financial contributions to the programme of about £1,000 per year.

The Hudson Trust continued to grow in financial strength, with the increasingly firm financial foundations allowing additional disbursements to support various Midshipmen studying at Oxford through grants for dissertation research, conferences and even Arabic lessons. This year also saw Sub-Lieutenant (later Commander) Conor O'Neill Royal Navy elected as a Junior Hudson Fellow immediately after his undergraduate graduation, allowing him to complete a period of postgraduate study as a probationer research student at Wadham College, researching the politics of Provisional Irish Republican Army strategy, before progressing his seagoing naval career.

The last of the 'Junior' Hudson Fellows was elected to study from September 2004. Instead of affiliating with St Antony's College she opted to rekindle the links between the Destroyer HMS *Exeter* and its namesake Exeter College. Lieutenant (later Commander) Elizabeth Cross (neé Squire) Royal Navy developed a thesis on 'Women of the Watch: A study of the social-psychological, human-resource, diversity and management issues that affect the retention of women in the Royal Navy'. Her efforts to intensify the relationship between the Royal Navy and the college came to fruition just after her fellowship was completed, when in October 2005 she organised at Exeter College a Trafalgar Night mess dinner, complete with Royal Marines band and attended by a large contingent from HMS *Exeter's* wardroom. As well as introducing academic fellows and students to the delights of after-dinner sea shanties (a longstanding Royal Navy tradition), the dinner tipped its hat to Guy with a dessert based on his favourite tipple: gin and tonic.

With the wording of Guy's bequest allowing considerable latitude for the trustees, 2005 saw the dropping of the term 'Junior' Hudson Fellow as it was felt that it was inappropriate. However, an 'Associate' Hudson Fellow was appointed in 2005 when Commodore Steven Jermy Royal Navy was granted an 18-month visiting fellowship based at Wolfson College, to research a book on strategy. With some in the Royal Navy now learning at first hand just how glacial progress in academia can be, his work came to fruition in 2011 when *Strategy for Action: Using Force Wisely in the 21st Century* was published by Knightstone.

The year 2005 also saw Captain Graham Peach Royal Navy elected as the Hudson Fellow, again to be based at St Antony's College. His research centred on maritime international disaster relief, building on his recent experience as Chief Staff Officer (Engineering) to Commander-in-Chief Fleet, where he had been responsible for coordinating the Royal Navy's response to the 2004 Boxing Day tsunami in the Indian Ocean. As well as representing St Antony's in their cricket 1st XI, he developed a number of papers and presentations on disaster relief from a maritime perspective. At the end of his studies his papers were given a wide distribution both within the United Kingdom and at the United Nations headquarters in New York, where they greatly added to understanding of how the maritime environment can be used to aid disaster response.

Although not financially supported by the Hudson Trust, the United States Navy continued to send USN Hudson Fellows. Captain Thomas Crompton Jr USN in 2005 studied global maritime security, to be succeeded at St Antony's College by Commander (later Captain) Donald Braswell. However, Commander Braswell had been accepted at St Antony's as a Senior Academic Member, rather than a Visiting Research Fellow, due to his lack of seniority, which was considered by the college to be a deviation from the terms of its agreement with Washington that candidates would always be officers with significant career potential who had already reached senior rank.

These first years of development and affiliation of serving naval academics at the university had seen many wonderful research successes, as well as a few hiccups in the relationship between St Antony's College and the Hudson Fellowship. Some St Antony's governing body Fellows had been cautious of having serving military officers in college whilst the country was at war, and they discussed a motion that would potentially have suspended the fellowship. However, some internal deconfliction within St Antony's allowed the voices of all sides to be heard, the internationally egalitarian status of the college to be upheld, and the fellows to continue their vital and rather timely research.

The Royal Navy Hudson Fellow for 2006 was also affected by the strictures of St Antony's College. The Royal Navy's preferred candidate was Lieutenant Commander Nigel Dawson, but his candidature was rejected by the college; the reasons cited were firstly his lack of seniority by rank, and also that only one candidate had been submitted for consideration (as opposed to the previous system whereby the college would have a choice of three nominations). The trustees of Hudson's legacy saw the issue of St Antony's insisting only on receiving 'senior' officers potentially leading to the trust educating 'yesterday's men' instead of the leaders of tomorrow, and a period of negotiation was commenced to manage the expectations of both parties. In a welcome development for the Royal Navy fellowship, agreement was reached with St Antony's College that instead of proposing three officers, nomination could be reduced to 'one well screened candidate', restoring the college as the Hudson Fellows' preferred location. However, for the year of 2006 Lieutenant Commander Dawson was affiliated to Exeter College, which was delighted to welcome him to succeed Lieutenant Cross.

The same year saw two further positive developments for Guy's legacy, with five Royal Navy barristers following in Guy's legal footsteps by receiving substantial support from the trust to undertake a course in international law at Mansfield College. The Hudson committee also achieved legal agreement with the university trustees that the Hudson Fund could be used 'for the direct or indirect benefit of Royal Navy or Royal Marine Officers at the University'. This extension of the remit of the fund granted Guy's trustees significantly enhanced flexibility as they sought to ensure his wishes for the further education of Royal Navy and Royal Marines officers were fulfilled.

By this time the sustainable income of the fund had reached £23,000 per year, allowing significant grants to be made to 18 individual URNU students (exceeding £5,000 in 2006/7) as well as payment of the Hudson Fellows' fees and associated research grants. Once further disbursements to the Codrington Library, the Oxford University Strategic Studies Group and the Changing Character of War programme were paid, the balance of annual income remained available for broader academic engagement including bringing some of the world's leading maritime academics to Oxford to present to both officer trainees and the wider university audience. The speaker at the recently instituted Guy Hudson annual dinner was the renowned Professor Geoffrey Till, who had two years earlier released the first edition of his seminal work on Seapower.

Lieutenant Commander Dawson completed his research into piracy, which he was later to put to considerable effect when working with the

EU mission to Somalia, to be replaced by Colonel (later Major General) Timothy Bevis Royal Marines, who was selected by the Hudson trustees from a list of 12 candidates (the fellowship by now being very popular) as the sole preferred nomination to be put to St Antony's College.

Researching what was probably the most politicised topic chosen to date, Colonel Bevis completed a paper titled 'Has New Labour Delivered Defence Forces for an Ethical Foreign Policy?' The complete script was submitted to the Ministry of Defence for approval before public release, but approval was unexpectedly withheld. Following a number of discussions between the trustees, who were very keen to ensure academic freedom of expression, and the Ministry's reviewers, Colonel Bevis' paper was eventually published internally to the Royal Navy as what is known as a Green Paper. In the autumn of 2007, reflecting the increasing profile of the fellowship, the speaker at Hudson's annual lecture (which now preceded the annual dinner) was Admiral Sir Jonathan Band, the First Sea Lord, who spoke about 'the role of navies in a risky globalised world'.

Colonel Bevis was succeeded as Hudson Fellow by Commander Jeff Short Royal Navy, who researched the somewhat less controversial but equally important topic of 'Recruiting, Retention and Reputation in the post-9/11 era: Implications for the UK Armed Forces'. Along with Commander Jeffrey Marshall US Navy, who was Washington's representative for 2008/9, Commander Short embarked on a significant programme of reaching out to the wider Oxford community through various strategic study societies as well as attending the Oxford Union. This naval outreach to the wider Oxford academic community included a wonderful after-dinner speech by Admiral Sir Mark Stanhope KCB OBE, then Commander-in-Chief Fleet, delivered at the annual Hudson memorial dinner. Using his acquired breadth of perspective, and reflecting Guy's penchant for a tipple, Commander Short then developed, rewrote, honed and critiqued much of his thesis within the bowels of Oxford's finest public house, the Rose and Crown, generously located only 100 yards from the back entrance to St Antony's College.

The year 2009 saw two Royal Navy Hudson Fellows: Captain (later Commodore) Martin Atherton Royal Navy undertook a 'short' fellowship at Christ Church, and, starting in Michaelmas term, Commander John Cunningham Royal Navy completed a full academic year at St Antony's. The United States were represented by Captain William Park, who focussed his research on 'The Mafia and the Mullah: Counternarcotics, counterinsurgency and realpolitik in Afghanistan'. In a tip of the hat to Guy's Coastal Forces heritage and the source of Guy's DSC protecting the flanks of D-Day, the annual Hudson lecture this year was given by Major General Andrew Salmon, the Commandant General Royal Marines, on the theme of the future utility of amphibious warfare.

The high esteem of the Hudson Fellowship became further evident in 2010 when the Commander-in-Chief Fleet, Admiral Trevor Soar KCB OBE, gave the after-dinner address at the annual Hudson memorial dinner. This was during the tenure as Hudson Fellow of Commodore (later Rear Admiral) Tom Karsten, who researched the geopolitics of the Arctic region. He was succeeded at St Antony's by Commodore Neil Brown, who, like Guy, was both a Royal Navy officer and a lawyer. Commodore Brown's research into the law of armed conflict led to the first major seminar sponsored by the Guy Hudson Memorial Trust, with legal students from the University of Oxford combining with a team from the University of Reading to arrange a witness seminar on the UK's 'Operation *Palliser*' millennium intervention in Sierra Leone. Oral histories were provided by, among others, General Sir David Richards (who in 2000 had been the Land Component Commander in Sierra Leone before going on to be Chief of the Defence Staff), and Admiral Sir Mark Stanhope (who had been the Maritime Component Commander off Sierra Leone before becoming First Sea Lord).

The United States Navy continued to send senior officers as its Hudson Fellows, with 2010's Captain Timothy Trampenau being relieved in September 2011 by Commander Tracey Vincent US Navy. Commander Vincent's research linked with that of the new Royal Navy Hudson Fellow, Commodore Keith Winstanley, culminating in them delivering a joint seminar on 'The Iranian Navy: Strategy, expansion and soft power' together with 'Maritime Security in the Indian Ocean'. Another highlight of 2011's fellowships was the address at the annual Hudson lecture by Admiral Gary Roughead, the 29th Chief of Naval Operations of the United States Navy, with the after-dinner reply given by Professor Andrew Hamilton, Vice-Chancellor of the University of Oxford.

Brigadier Richard Spencer OBE Royal Marines and Captain Bill Combes US Navy were the 2012 Hudson Fellows at St Antony's College before Commander Bobby Baker US Navy arrived for Michaelmas term to study the European Union Naval Force's Operation *Atalanta* (countering piracy off Somalia). Commander Baker was joined at the start of Hilary term 2014 by Captain Jon White Royal Navy, who was studying maritime security off Sierra Leone. Both fellows were then joined in Trinity term 2014 by Lieutenant Commander Ryan Coatalen-Hodgson Royal Navy, who undertook a short-term Hudson Fellowship as he prepared for an assignment to Russia as the UK's Assistant Naval Attaché in Moscow.

The autumn of 2014 saw the most senior serving Hudson Fellow take up his post, when Lieutenant General Sir David Capewell KCB OBE joined St Antony's. Sir David had until his fellowship been serving as the UK's Chief of Joint Operations, and seized the opportunity of a year at Oxford to develop his thoughts and reflections on military command and control in recent operations, going on to become a senior mentor to the UK's Higher Command and Staff Course. Both Sir David and Commander Joseph Gagliano US Navy were, like all Hudson Fellows since 2003, affiliated to the Changing Character of War programme, where Sir David remains a Senior Fellow.

Michaelmas term 2015 saw another lawyer follow in Guy's footsteps to Oxford, when Captain (now Commodore) Rob Wood Royal Navy joined St Antony's College, producing a peer-reviewed paper on 'The Legal Dimensions of Hybrid Warfare', prior to taking up an assignment as Commodore Naval Legal Services. Whilst at Oxford, Captain Wood linked up with helicopter pilot Commander (now Captain) Matt Schnappauf US

Navy to use their Hudson Fellowships to develop aspects of UK–US interoperability, which was becoming a key operational development area as the new British aircraft carrier HMS *Queen Elizabeth* was fitting out ready for sea trials. A short fellowship was also undertaken that year by Lieutenant Colonel Aran Jess Royal Marines.

Lieutenant Commander Matt Offord PhD Royal Navy assumed the Hudson Fellowship between September 2016 and July 2017, studying naval leadership techniques with a focus on the particularly unusual subject of resistance to leadership, or how subordinates can try to frustrate or disrupt the plans of their superiors. Lieutenant Commander Offord worked alongside Captain Justin Orlich USN, who as the US Navy Hudson Fellow focussed his research on 'Russian Military Intervention in the 21st Century' before taking up an assignment as the United States' Naval Attaché to Canada.

Twenty years after the first Hudson Fellow arrived at St Antony's, Michaelmas term 2017 saw Captain Chris O'Flaherty Royal Navy take up the fellowship in order to study naval mines as instruments of foreign policy, publishing in the *St Antony's International Review* a paper on 'The Naval Minefield of Customary International Humanitarian Law', as well as presenting his experiences of UK–US joint naval operations to the Oxford University Strategic Studies Group. He was joined by Commander Justin Harts US Navy, who conducted a suite of investigations into US Navy surface warfare officer training as well as bringing to Oxford his considerable experience of operations in the South China Sea. Maximising the benefits intended by Guy, both officers travelled together to mainland Europe to deliver presentations to NATO counterparts, thus extending the breadth of recipients of Guy's legacy.

The Guy Hudson Memorial Trust (or GHMT as it is now known) has developed a sustainable income of over £30,000 per year. This very firm financial position is facilitating one full-time Royal Navy Hudson Fellow per year, occasional short-term Royal Navy Hudson Fellowships, and an annual Hudson lecture, usually delivered by very senior military or academic personalities and held at a prestigious Oxford college, followed by an annual Guy Hudson memorial dinner, addressed by a wide variety of senior guest speakers. These last two events form a core element of the annual programme for Midshipmen of the Oxford University Royal Naval Unit, ensuring the benefit of Guy's legacy is shared annually among the approximately 60 young naval officers at the university.

These young officers further benefit from many disbursements from Guy's memorial funds, which facilitate numerous group training activities ranging from visiting Formula One teams to ballroom dancing lessons. Guy's legacy also permits the allocation of specific grants to individual Midshipmen who have a particular need for financial assistance with their studies. In consequence to this wide variety of activities funded by Guy's legacy, the number of beneficiaries over the first 20 years since his death must be measured in the high hundreds. And, with Guy's Hudson Fellowship brand also shared across the Atlantic with the US Navy, his legacy can truly be described as international.

Guy Hudson also left further standing legacies. Sponsored by his trustees, the Hudson Memorial Trophy is a 12-inch silver model of MTB 77, in which Hudson was First Lieutenant, and is presented annually 'for academic and naval excellence' to Oxford University's best University Royal Naval Unit student in the year, generally a third-year who has recently graduated. It was first presented in 1998, to Midshipman Helen Keron Royal Naval Reserve, and has been presented annually ever since.

Away from the university, Guy has left his mark on the fighting arms of the Royal Navy. His development of duties and tactics for the Surface Force Direction Officer, who directed maritime combat from an 'operations room' remote from the bridge of a warship, marked the beginning of a shift in the conduct of naval warfare that persists today. The Royal Navy's Action Information Organisation, which was developed in part by Guy, along with Lieutenant Phillip Lee, is still in use – with the same name. In their report of March 1945, it was stated that:

> The Action Information Organisation, with its plots, Radar displays and system of correlating all information received regarding the enemy, provides the Command with the information and data necessary for interception and the tactical disposing of units for a co-ordinated attack and enables a Senior Officer to place his attached forces in the most suited tactical position for a co-ordinated attack on the enemy from two or more sectors, having complete control of movements of own forces until the moment of engaging the enemy arrives.[19]

This description would not be unfamiliar to a 21st century naval warrior. Going into combat, the captain of all modern Royal Navy warships from Frigate upwards will, on the vast majority of occasions, be found fighting their ship from an operations room in the heart of the ship, of a layout Guy would probably recognise, and with a flow of tactical information nearly identical to Guy's pioneering drills. Despite the technologies being somewhat more advanced, should Guy ever look down on such a ship he would see an officer (now known as a Principal Warfare Officer), surrounded by a refined Action Information Organisation, fighting the ship in the same way that Guy fought from a Captain-class Frigate in 1944.

---

[19] *Coastal Forces Periodic Review*, January–March 1945, p.51.

Epilogue

Richard Guy Ormonde Hudson was an ordinary middle-class boy, from a successful business family, brought up in a city far from the sea and schooled even further from the maritime environment which came to dominate his war. His love of being afloat stemmed from occasional trips to his extended family in Ireland, where he learnt to sail in small boats along the rocky west coast.

This affection for the sea and his ability as a sailor were to prove of huge benefit to his country. After starting a degree at one of the most prestigious universities in the world, Guy's patriotism overrode his personal ambition and he volunteered to serve his nation in the Royal Navy's fight against the Axis forces of Germany and Italy. Eight months later he experienced the horrors of war when service as a coder in the Destroyer HMS *Sikh* saw him witness the sinking of the great German battleship *Bismarck*, and his ship was ordered not to stop and pick up German survivors due to the presence of an enemy U-Boat. Men of his own age drowned right in front of him, in the name of war. This event was the seed of memories that were to haunt him for the rest of his life, probably germinating into what modern medicine refers to as Post-Traumatic Stress Disorder, or PTSD.

His potential as a significant contributor to the British war effort was recognised early on, and Guy was guided through the Royal Naval Volunteer Reserve scheme for commissioning able sailors for the duration of hostilities only. Despatched to the Mediterranean as a young Sub-Lieutenant, he was appointed to a sickly ship which rarely sailed, and he was absent from the second traumatic event of his career when his former ship, HMS *Sikh,* was attacked and sunk by Axis forces off Tobruk. His fellow Motor Torpedo Boat (MTB) officers had been unable to protect his former shipmates whilst Guy was repairing defects back at the British naval base in Alexandria; Guy had lost close friends to enemy action, and he had been unable to help them.

His war improved somewhat when he was assigned to a more modern and much more reliable MTB based in Malta, but drink had by this time started to get the better of him and he was injured 'tripping over a carpet', trying to use a pane of glass to break his fall. Despite a deep laceration to his hand, he continued to serve with his fellow small-ship warriors and saw sustained action against Italian and German forces whilst forward based in Sousse on the Tunisian coast. Taking part in a number of daring raids, he endured seeing another fellow sailor succumb to the waves when trying to conduct a night rescue of colleagues from a grounded MTB right under the muzzles of Italian guns, going on to bury close colleagues from other MTBs who failed to survive their own raids on enemy shipping. However, he did achieve his own little victories against the enemy, driving his MTB on her silent engine into an enemy-held harbour and torpedoing enemy barges anchored under the supposed protection of enemy guns, before crash-starting 4,050 horsepower of main engines to get out of the induced mêlée very quickly indeed.

Returned to the United Kingdom to recover from his worsening injury, he turned his sharp brain to developing battle-winning tactics that were to make a huge difference to the Allied successes at Normandy. Alongside his great friend Lieutenant Phillip Lee, Guy's embracing of the modern technology of radar to vector his colleagues in MTBs into near-perfect torpedo firing positions drove the German forces further and further away from the Allied landings until Guy's tactics, combined with the incredible bravery of all the ships' companies in his sector, had comprehensively secured the vital eastern flank. His tactics were so successful that other Allies adopted them, the United States Navy using them with considerable success on the opposite maritime flank off Cherbourg. By the end of this phase of fighting, Guy's contribution towards Allied victory was deemed so significant that he was awarded the Distinguished Service Cross. But whilst earning this recognition he had also created for himself yet more memories of wounded colleagues, badly damaged ships, and close friends under his radar control who were never to return from that battlefield. What he had seen whilst fighting the enemy could never be unseen.

Having fallen in love with Sylvia, the attractive daughter of a solicitor, he married, demobilised and resumed his studies to qualify as a lawyer. However, he had by then developed a strong penchant for gin and tonic, which was his escape from his battlefield memories. His signature gin-based drink, with which he would welcome anyone who visited, was his Hudson Heart-Starter. Increasingly aided by this tipple, he enjoyed many years of happiness with Sylvia, providing a counterpoint to the memories of enemy action he was so desperate to suppress.

Often working with his father-in-law, Guy built a successful legal practice whilst succumbing ever more to the demon of alcohol. Eventually his drinking came to dominate his life, to the detriment of both his work and his childless marriage. Increasingly consumed by alcohol, Guy drove Sylvia to separate from him just after their silver wedding anniversary (at which Guy was drunk). His life now at a low ebb, he moved to Devon to be near his parents and saw his legal practice collapse, followed by losing his legal licence for failing to keep proper accounts. He was near to bankruptcy, drink was destroying him and he was paralysed by the fear created by large debts. But, like many veterans of his generation, he was too proud to seek the help he needed. He was a caring son, but he was failing to care for himself.

His saviour proved to be the receptionist at his local medical practice. Guy met Patricia whenever he collected his parents' medication, and Pat eventually persuaded Guy to face his demons, see a doctor and dry himself out. Guy and Pat married, settled together and shared 20 years of wonderful happiness, during which Guy turned his intellect to amassing a considerable fortune by playing the stock market. Guy was back riding along on the crest of life's wave, thoroughly enjoying life as a husband, stepfather and granddad.

Such wonderful waves rarely last for ever, eventually crashing onto shore.

Guy's tragic return to the depths occurred when Pat was taken from him by a debilitating series of medical issues. With his rock now absent from his life, Guy immediately turned back to drink, which was to be his final downfall.

He did again find friendship, and happiness, when a former acquaintance started to pick him out of his latest maelstrom. Some of his friends questioned how true this happiness was, when his apparent angel started to guide Guy towards sharing much of his wealth with her. But Guy was happy in himself, once again aided by his favourite tipple. By early evening on many days he would be well over the drink-drive limit for alcohol, with yet more alcohol still to flow. His judgement potentially clouded, and under the spell of his new companion, he was three days away from signing a new will which would have reallocated much of his fortune away from his intended charitable legacy.

Choking in exceptionally unfortunate circumstances, with his new companion unable to save him, Guy crossed the bar in 1995. Childless, he gave almost all his wealth to three charities, one of which is now his true lasting legacy. His memory lives on through the Guy Hudson Memorial Trust, for which this author is enormously grateful.

In the years since his death Guy has been the benefactor for 28 fellows at his former university, studying subjects ranging from piracy to people, and from maritime law to humanitarian relief. It is fitting that many of these fellows have been fellow lawyers, studying variations of the very subject that gave Guy his professional satisfaction. His enduring legacy has also helped many hundreds of undergraduate naval students to fund their studies and professional development, and the trust that bears his name has attracted some of the world's leading maritime experts and naval leaders to his former university. If Guy is now looking down on Oxford, he should smile with pride at what he has achieved.

The life of Richard Guy Ormonde Hudson reads like a rollercoaster of achievement, emotion, selflessness, success and tragedy. Like many of his generation he served his country with a vigour, dedication and focus that saved his nation in its time of need. Like many of his generation he then had to deal with the memories thus created — and he tried to cope on his own, not wishing to burden others with what he may have assumed would not be of interest to them. After a gentle cognitive descent that even those closest to him failed to notice, it was one person, Pat, who managed to break through the veneer of a self-reliant sailor in order to act as his compass. He stood on firm, sober ground for 20 good years before being pulled back into the abyss.

What probably consumed Guy during his low years is what we now call PTSD, something for which help can be provided when sought. Guy came from a generation that barely knew about the reality of what traumatic memories can do to otherwise sound minds. With good fortune, perhaps others can use modern hindsight to thus learn from Guy's life. Not only is it hoped that the Hudson Fellows can continue their education on account of the Guy Hudson Memorial Trust; it is also hoped that very many more people can learn from Guy's rollercoaster life to keep friendships close, and to seek help when it is needed. I hope this book may provide that inspiration.

LIST OF SOURCES

The secretary and trustees of the Guy Hudson Memorial Trust:

- Lieutenant Will Jones Royal Navy
- Professor Christopher Davis
- Mr Jeremy Lee (memories of Guy Hudson, the setting up of the Guy Hudson Memorial Fund, and Hudson's legacy)
- Minutes of Guy Hudson Memorial Trust committee meetings (these minutes informed much of the narrative in the chapter 'Hudson's Legacy')

Genealogy research supported by Findmypast.co.uk

The Government Probate Service (online) provided wills and grants of probate for:

- James Ormonde Hudson
- Richard Guy Ormonde Hudson
- Richard Henry Hudson
- Sylvia Mary Hudson
- Patricia Jesse Rowland Hudson

Investigative assistance provided by the enquiries services of:

- Birmingham Municipal Museum (location of Lieutenant Richard Hudson's Waterloo Medal)
- National Maritime Museum (declining the gift of the painting *Sinking of the Bismarck*)
- Royal National Lifeboat Institution
- Solicitors Regulation Authority (circumstances of Guy Hudson being struck off in 1973)

- St John's College, University of Oxford
- St Antony's College, University of Oxford
- University of Oxford trustees
- Queen's Chapel of the Savoy, London (Guy and Sylvia's wedding)
- North Devon Records Office, Barnstaple

North Devon Records Office, Barnstaple Library:

- *North Devon Journal-Herald*, 28 December 1973 (Guy Hudson's striking off)
- *North Devon Journal*, 10 August 1995 (Guy Hudson's inquest, and his (alleged) third engagement)

Personal interviews:

- Hon. Michael Cochrane OBE
- Mr Christopher Corfield (memories of Guy and Patricia Hudson)
- Mrs Veryan Green (memories of Guy and Sylvia Hudson during their marriage, and the circumstances of their parting ways)
- Captain Peter Hore Royal Navy (the setting up of the Guy Hudson Memorial Fund)
- Mrs Sally Barbier (memories of Guy Hudson and his family throughout his second marriage, and the circumstances of his death)

Personal letters:

- Mr Christopher Price
- Mrs Yolande Butler

Correspondence with Hudson Fellows (informing much of the narrative in 'Hudson's Legacy'):

- Vice Admiral Timothy Laurence KCBO CB ADC
- Rear Admiral Neil Latham CBE
- Commodore Guy Challands Royal Navy

- Commodore Rob Wood Royal Navy
- Captain Graham Peach Royal Navy
- Captain Graham Wiltshire Royal Navy
- Commander (now Professor) Steven Haines Royal Navy
- Commander Justin Harts United States Navy
- Commander Jeff Short Royal Navy
- Commander Elizabeth Squire Royal Navy
- Lieutenant Commander Matt Offord PhD Royal Navy

The *London Gazette*.

Maritime Warfare Centre, Fareham:

- BR 1736 (3/50): The Chase and Sinking of the *Bismarck*. Naval Staff History, Second World War, Battle Summary No. 5 (this official summary was used to verify the account of the sinking of the *Bismarck*, including details of other ships' activities and the presence of a German U-Boat)
- BR 1736 (37): The Campaign in North-West Europe June 1944– May 1945. Naval Staff History, Second World War, Battle Summary No. 49 (descriptions of the MTB actions on the eastern flank of the D-Day landings)

The National Archives:

- Service records and S206 reports for Richard Guy Ormonde Hudson
- HMS *Hornet* Recommendation for Mention in Despatches, 15 September 1944
- Citation for Distinguished Service Cross (Register Number H&A 980/44, 30 October 1944), with enclosures
- Commander-in-Chief Portsmouth's 6011/0/9684/3, 18 September 1944 (German evacuation of Le Havre by sea).

Naval Historical Branch, Portsmouth:

- *Coastal Forces Periodic Review* (CB 04272 (14), and BR 1874 (14)), various (this series of documents was invaluable in providing details of control ship tactics, as well as summaries of significant MTB actions)
- Navy lists
- Coastal Forces Historical Notes, Second World War (compiled by 'Information Room, Historical Section, 1958')
- Commander-in-Chief Mediterranean War Diary (duplicate), May–September 1943
- Senior Officer, 7th MTB Flotilla's 7F/90/138, 15 May 1943 (report of Operation *Retribution*)
- Senior Officer, 7th MTB Flotilla's 7F/91/138, 15 May 1943 (summary of operations whilst based at Sousse)
- Ship's information cards for MTBs (these documents provide shipping dates, locations and refit periods)
- Report on Operation *Overlord*, Portsmouth Command (Coastal Forces Enclosure), 765/0/5, 12 September 1944 (this document provided much of the information on Coastal Forces engagements off Le Havre and Cap d'Antifer used for the chapter 'The Night Fight')
- Office of the Commander-in-Chief Portsmouth's 0/0302/76/31, 30 May 1944 (Operation *Neptune*, Portsmouth Operational Orders; ON Portsmouth 1: The Defence of the Western Wall; this document provided disposition and tactical information for 'The Night Fight' and 'Warm Waters – Hot Engagements')

Rugby School archives:

- *The Meteor* (school magazine), 1935–1940
- The reports of the Rugby School Natural History Society for 1936, 1937 and 1938

Internet documents:

- Letters of David Edmond Cole-Hamilton, the First Lieutenant on HMS *Sikh*, published by the Forces War Records Archive at https://www.forces-war-records.co.uk/blog/2015/01/15/eye-witness-account-of-the-sinking-of-the-bismarck (accessed 14 September 2018)
- Obituary of Sir James Eberle, *The Times*, 4 July 2018. Available at https://www.thetimes.co.uk/article/admiral-sir-james-eberle-obituary-tr8prj2hs (accessed 23 October 2018)

Published books:

Bulkley, Robert J. *At Close Quarters: PT Boats in the United States Navy*. Washington: Naval History Division, 1962

Chapman, Anthony. *The War of the Motor Gun Boats*. Barnsley: Praetorian Press, 2013

Cobb, David. *Profile Warship 7: HM MTB/Vosper 70ft*. Windsor: Profile, 1971

Cooper, Bryan. *The Battle of the Torpedo Boats*. London: Macdonald, 1970

Jefferson, David. *Coastal Forces at War: Royal Navy 'Little Ships' in World War 2*. Sparkford: Haynes, 1996

Konstam, Angus. *British Motor Torpedo Boats 1939-45*. Oxford: Osprey, 2003

Lavery, Brian. *Hostilities Only*. London: Conway, 2004

Menzies, Ian. *We Fought Them on the Seas*. North Reading, MA: Cheshire Press, 2012

Pickles, Harold. *Untold Stories of Small Boats at War*. Durham: Pentland Press, 1994

Pope, Dudley. *Flag 4*. London: William Kimber, 1954

Reynolds, L C, and H F Cooper. *MTBs at War*. Gloucester: Sutton, 1999

Roskill, S W. *The War at Sea 1939–1945*, vol. III. London: HMSO, 1961

Scott, Peter. *The Battle of the Narrow Seas*. London: Country Life, 1945

Williamson, Gordon. *E-Boat vs MTB: The English Channel 1941–1945*. Oxford: Osprey, 2011

Appendix A:

Hudson Fellows, Junior Hudson Fellows, Associate Hudson Fellows and Their Colleges 1997–2017

---❧☙❧---

1997	Captain G D Challands Royal Navy, St Antony's
1998	Commodore T J H Laurence MVO Royal Navy, St Antony's
1999	Captain G Wiltshire Royal Navy, St Antony's
2000	Commander A C Ashcroft Royal Navy, Christ Church
2000	Commander S W Haines Royal Navy, St Antony's
2001	Commodore N D Latham Royal Navy, St Antony's
2002	Commander N S Roberts Royal Navy, St Antony's
2003	Commander M Mason Royal Navy, St Antony's
2003	Sub-Lieutenant Conor O'Neill Royal Navy, Wadham
2004	Lieutenant E Cross Royal Navy, Exeter
2005	Captain G L Peach Royal Navy, St Antony's
2005	Commodore S Jermy Royal Navy, Wolfson
2006	Lieutenant Commander N J F Dawson Royal Navy, Exeter
2007	Colonel T J Bevis Royal Marines, St Antony's
2008	Commander J J Short Royal Navy, St Antony's
2009	Captain M Atherton Royal Navy, Christ Church
2009	Commander J Cunningham Royal Navy, St Antony's
2010	Commodore T M Karsten Royal Navy, St Antony's
2010	Commodore N L Brown Royal Navy, St Antony's
2011	Commodore K Winstanley Royal Navy, St Antony's
2012	Brigadier R Spencer OBE Royal Marines, St Antony's
2014	Captain J A P White Royal Navy, St Antony's
2014	Lieutenant Commander R Coatalen-Hodgson Royal Navy, St Antony's
2014	Lieutenant General Sir D Capewell KCB OBE, St Antony's
2015	Captain R Wood Royal Navy, St Antony's
2015	Lieutenant Colonel A Jess Royal Marines, St Antony's
2016	Lieutenant Commander M Offord PhD Royal Navy, St Antony's
2017	Captain C P J O'Flaherty Royal Navy, St Antony's

Appendix B:

Guy Hudson Memorial Trophy Winners 1998–2018

'For Academic and Naval Excellence'

1998   Mid Helen Keron RNR
1999   Mid Jeremy Westhead RNR
2000   Mid Neil King RNR
2001   Mid John Selden RNR
2002   Mid Jenifer Parkins RNR
2003   Mid Alistair Ferguson RNR
2004   Mid John Adair RNR
2005   Mid Louise Eggett RNR
2006   Mid Karina Smith RNR
2007   Mid Thomas Shinner RNR
2008   Mid Duncan White RNR
2009   Mid Kelly Smith RNR
2010   Mid Matthew Irwin RNR
2011   Mid Jonathan Ho RNR
2012   Mid Michael Juniper RNR
2013   Mid Rosie Gibbs RNR
2014   Mid David Griffith-Jones RNR
2015   Mid James Sinclair RNR
2016   Mid Jessie Tucker RNR
2017   Mid Benjamin Clarke RNR
2018   Mid John Hawke RNR